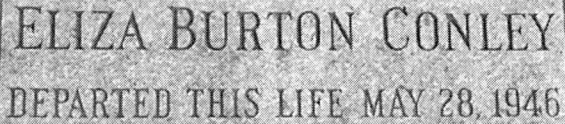

ELIZA BURTON CONLEY
DEPARTED THIS LIFE MAY 28, 1946
ATTORNEY AT LAW.
ONLY WOMAN EVER ADMITTED TO
THE UNITED STATES SUPREME COURT

HELENA CONLEY
FLOATING VOICE
WYANDOTTE NATIONAL BURYING GROUND
"CURSED BE THE VILLIAN THAT
MOLEST THEIR GRAVES"

IDA CONLEY
DEPARTED THIS LIFE
OCT. 6, 1948

A Luis Moro Production

Whispers Like Thunder

A True Native American Story

The three Conley Sisters fought the U.S Government with guns, axes, and the law to protect their Wyandot Ancestors graves

Written by
Trip Brooks
Luis A. Moro

WHISPERS LIKE THUNDER
A True Native American Story

The true story of the three Conley sisters who fought the United States Government with guns, the law and their spirits to prevent their Ancestors from being removed from their final resting place in Heron Cemetery.

Original Screenplay by:

*Trip Brooks
&
Luis Moro*

A Luis Moro Production

"YOU TRESPASS AT YOUR OWN PERIL."

Lyda Conley was the *first Native American woman* to plead a case in the United States Supreme Court.

Lyda along with her sisters, **Ida Conley** and **Helena Conley** built a 6' x 8' shack over their ancestors graves.

They then built a crude fence around what came to be known as Fort Conley, padlocked the gate, and posted a sign that read, "Trespass at your Peril."

The sisters guarded Fort Conley night and day for over four years and their fight continued for almost forty years.

"I will stand guard over the grave of my mother with a gun if I have to."
Lyda Conley

This made for film script is an action driven drama based on a true story. It was written with permission and support from the Wyandot Nation of Kansas.

Copyright © 2017 Trip Brooks, Luis Moro, L.A. Moro, Luis Moro Productions, Inc. All rights reserved. Except as permitted under the U.S. Copyright Act of 1976, no part of this publication may be reproduced, distributed, or transmitted in any form or by any means, or stored in a database or retrieval system, without prior written permission of the publisher Transparent Technologies, Inc.

ISBN-13: 978-1979445207

ISBN-10: 1979445206

Thank you to those who continue to champion "Whispers Like Thunder".

The Wyandot Nation of Kansas
Janith English, Chief of the Wyandot Nation of Kansas
Claire-Michelle Young
Robert Roeland

Dedication

Dedicated to all the Spirits of the living and dead who have felt the pain of unjust deaths, persecution, and the suppression of human dignity by the few who continue to rule by force, whether murder, violence or unjust laws.

Synopsis

Whispers Like Thunder is an empowering uplifting story that passes on the undeniable spirit of Native Americans against all odds for generations to come.

Whispers Like Thunder is the true story of three Native American sisters who fought the U.S. government to save their ancestors sacred burial ground for almost forty years. The Conley sisters began their revolt in 1906 to prevent the U.S Government from following through on the sale of their ancestor's final resting place.

This is a compelling story of Native Americans being expelled from their own lands in the name of civilization, business and raw human greed. The U.S. Government sold the Native American cemetery completely ignoring a U.S. treaty with the Wyandot Nation.

As soon as the three Conley sisters realized that the sale was pending they announced they would protect the graves of their ancestors until their last breath. Forthwith, they marched to the cemetery and built a six by eight foot one room frame shack in the center of their ancestral resting place and occupied it for over four years.

No one would represent them in court. So Lyda an attorney began to fight their battle in the halls of justice. Her sisters, Helena and Ida worked to support them while living in the cemetery. As they used their voices, swung their fists and pulled their triggers, the government increased its legal, physical and relentless might to expel them. The U.S. government came after them with U.S. Marshals, police, military and the abuse of law. Others used thug force and constant varied attacks. But the three Native American sisters never gave up.

In a time when Native Americans and women had any rights, respect or a voice, the three Conley sisters proved that our spirits continue to live through those who come after us. Lyda Conley became the first Native American woman to plead a case in front of the Supreme Court.

WHISPERS LIKE THUNDER

Written by:
Trip Brooks
&
Luis Moro

Based on an original story by:

Trip Brooks
&
Shelly Young

**"All Native American scenes
spoken in the original Wyandot language."**

A Luis Moro Production
Contact: 301.728.0851
Luis@ MoroFilms.com

                              FADE IN:

BLACK SCREEN, THUNDEROUS WINDS APPROACH.

                  FLOATING VOICE (V.O.)
        I will be the bearer of the words
        you speak, and your daughters the
        bearer of yours. Until there is
        nothing left to say. I am Floating
        Voice.

CLOUDS ROLL IN AN APPROACHING THUNDERSTORM

                  FLOATING VOICE (V.O) (cont'd)
        I am everlasting and the wind that
        now scatters our spirits will one
        day lift us high upon its wings and
        return us home.

                                                DISSOLVE TO:

EXT. HURON CEMETARY. NIGHT - THE YEAR IS 1906

A series of GRAVE STONES; ANDREW WHITMAN CONLEY, 1875. ELIZA ZANE CONLEY, JULY 11, 1879. FLOATING VOICE, has no dates.

RAIN soaks a COURT ORDER, DATED 1906 TO EVACUATE HURON CEMETERY; it washes away in a muddy rain of river.

Darkness prevails as wind driven rain pelts a small wooden shack. DARK FIGURES, begin to appear and surround the small structure. In one movement the men attack the shack with picks and sledgehammers caught in the faint thundering light. Boards are ripped out and others splintered into pieces.

The door to the shack bursts open and two female figures, their long hair and dresses mixing together as they tackle the bodies in front of them.

Rain, mud, cursing and bodies mix in a hysterical dance around the shack.

                  DARK FIGURE #1
        What the hell was that!

                  DARK FIGURE #2
        Over there...look out.

A board slaps the water as Figure #1 rolls out of the way.

A woman's hair is pulled and she falls forward into the mud. From the blackened face, white teeth glow as they find their mark in a third DARK FIGURES arm.

DARK FIGURE #3
                 They're eating me!

The Dark Figures wrestle the women to their feet. The women
kick and claw as the men hold them tight. Other men continue
the devastation on the shack.

The red and white flash of a shotgun is followed a second
later by a thunderous clap as it rips in front of the bodies.

Everyone freezes, as the men release the women. The rain
begins to wash away the mud revealing the fighting women's
faces.

                                          FADE OUT.

INT. LOCOMOTIVE TRAIN - JANUARY, 1910

The Thundering roar of the iron dragon dominates the plains.

Lena sleeps, as her head is bouncing against the window. We
see the turn of the century evolving as the west meets east
in the landscape. Lyda sits across from Lena, writing notes.

                    I.T. MARTIN (O.S.)
                 Miss Conley?

Lyda turns to find, I.T. MARTIN, a young man.

                    LYDA
                 I'm Lyda Conley.

                    I.T. MARTIN
                 I'm I.T. Martin from Kansas
                 Magazine. I've being sent to
                 Washington, to follow your case.

Lyda turns to her note book, with no time to waste.

                    LYDA
                 It's not my case.

                    I.T. MARTIN
                 May I ask you a few questions?

                    LYDA
                 You can ask me whatever you like.
                 You just may not like what I say.

I.T. Martin takes a cautious seat next to Lena.

                    I.T. MARTIN
          My notes say your name is Eliza
          Burton Conley? Graduated 1902,
          Kansas City College of Law? Is that
          correct?

                    LYDA
          I'm a lawyer, well beyond graduate.
          Eliza is my mother. My name is Lyda
          Conley and if my name appears any
          other way I'll sue you for
          defamation of character.

                    I.T. MARTIN
          No, no. I have it. I understand.
          Lyda. L..Y..D..A. You are on your
          way to our nations Supreme Court?
          Correct?

                    LYDA
          Excuse me.

                    I.T. MARTIN
          An, an... attorney must be admitted
          to practice in the Supreme Court.
          Huh, you are not... and, you are an
          Indian?

Lyda's focus now penetrates the young man.

                    LYDA
          I am willing to take the
          examination if I can find anyone
          who will stand and sponsor me. No
          lawyer could plead for the graves
          of my ancestors, our nations
          history as I can.

                    I.T. MARTIN
          Do you think you're going to win?

                    LYDA
          Ask my sister.

I.T. Martin nervously checks his notes.

                    I.T. MARTIN
          Um...are you afraid living in a
          cemetery?

                    LYDA
          Afraid of the dead? I sleep on the
          graves of my family. I sleep well.

                    I.T. MARTIN
          Thank you Miss Conley. I wish you
          the best.

I.T. Martin shakes Lyda's hand and stands. He looks at Lena,
her head is now flowing in unison with the waves of the
trains progress.

                    I.T. MARTIN (CONT'D) (cont'd)
          Doesn't that bother her?

                    LYDA
          Ask her.

Lena's eyes are wide open with a stunning smile, as if she
slept on clouds.

INT. WASHINGTON LAW OFFICE - DAY

A MIDDLE AGED couple enters a waiting room. Lyda is sitting
inside. A WHITE MAN exits an office as BRIAN LITTLETON
follows. Brian looks at the sign-in list.

                    BRIAN LITTLETON
          How can I help you?

The couple rises.

                    LYDA
          Excuse me. I've been next for two
          hours.

                    BRIAN LITTLETON
          In Washington we show respect to
          our elders.

The couple disappear into the office with Brian. Lyda sits
finding her own solace, with distance laughs from the office.

EXT. 1910 WASHINGTON, DC STREETS - CONTINUOUS

Lyda crosses Brian's name off a long list. She looks for her
next choice and starts walking against the winter wind.

Lyda's spirit and determination is renewed by the massive
Landmarks representing The United States of America.

Through the mist, The U.S. Capitol Building is revealed.

                    FLOATING VOICE (V.O.)
          A paragraph that would allow the
          United States government to sell
          the sacred Wyandot burial ground
          was hidden on page six hundred and
          sixty-five of a congressional
          Appropriations Bill. These few
          simple words awoke the spirits that
          were buried a thousand miles away.

INT. INDIAN LONGHOUSE - DAWN - THE YEAR IS 1842

A woman's hand, brown and calloused is clenched tight as a soft young female hand is placed upon it. Slowly, the fingers of the older hand are opened to reveal a simple river stone. The young hand re-closes the older fingers over the stone.

LITTLE BIRD ZANE, beautiful, twenties, with long black hair pulls an animal pelt over her mother RIVER SONG then stands.

Around them a sleeping community of, men, women, and children. Carefully, Little Bird makes her way outside.

EXT. 1906 CONLEY FAMILY HOME, KANSAS CITY MISSOURI - MORNING

A screen door slams open. LENA CONLEY, thirty, high top shoes and a dress far too large runs past LYDA CONLEY, thirty three who is sitting on the porch reading LAW BOOKS.

                    LENA
          We've got to go!

Lyda pulls her arm away and stops, sending Lena stumbling down the stairs.

                    LYDA
          Please Lena, I'm preparing a case.
          Look at you, you're not even
          dressed.

Lena looks down at her nightgown. She then runs back into the house and returns in a coat.

                    LENA
          I am now!

                    LYDA
          You've completely lost your mind.

Lena pulls her off the porch and down the street.

EXT. RIVER STEAMBOAT DOCK STATION - DAY

They stop at the river's edge as a transport boat waits.

LYDA
(Out of breath)
Lena, I'm not getting on this boat unless you tell me what is going on.

BOAT CAPTAIN (O.S.)
Any time now, ladies.

LENA
It won't make any sense if I tell you now.

LYDA
Nothing you do makes any sense.

Lena steps onto the boat and the BOAT CAPTAIN looks with disdain at her bed clothes showing under her coat. Lena raises her head a little higher and walks to the front.

The boat crosses the Missouri River. Large concrete, glass and brick buildings rise from the Kansas City hillside.

EXT. RIVER SHORELINE HILL SIDE - CONTINUOUS

The sisters arrive on the shore, Lena jumps off the boat running. She stops as Lyda begins a lazy walk behind her.

LENA
They're already there!

Lena begins running again. This time, Lyda rolls her eyes but catches her sister. They run along the shore for a hundred yards and start up a hill.

EXT. HURON CEMETARY - DAY

Out of breath, the sisters stop at the top of the hill. Three workers with shovels and JAMES WHITAKER, forty, tall, and thin, are walking toward the cemetary grounds.

The two sister's eyes are locked in a knowing stare, then Lyda turns to the men just as they step onto the cemetery.

LYDA
You there! What business do you have on these grounds?

The men with the shovels stop and turn, James keeps walking.

                  LENA
One more step and you might as well dig your own grave!

James turns, his cheeks flushed.

                JAMES WHITAKER
And who the hell are you?

The two sisters, shoulder to shoulder, walk forward.

                  LENA
We're Wayandot! Who the hell are you?

                JAMES WHITAKER
James Whitaker. I'm the man that the government sent to do the survey of this cemetery. I set many of the grave markers I'm about to remove.

                  LYDA
Whitaker, finally a face for the name.

                JAMES WHITAKER
This land is about to be sold and we're moving the bodies over to Quindaro Cemetery.

The two sisters continue walking forward as the workers step out of the way.

                  LYDA
Then I guess you'll have two more bodies to move. Not one soul or piece of soil is going to pass from this sacred ground as long as we are alive.

                JAMES WHITAKER
You'll get your out of the money. Now leave us be. Come on men, we've got a lot of work to do before dark.

The sisters turn and stare down the workers.

                    LENA
          You move onto this sacred ground
          and you will be haunted the rest of
          your days. The spirits of those
          resting here will rise up and find
          you.

The workers look at each other with wide eyes and back away quickly from the sisters, finally turning and running off.

                    JAMES WHITAKER
          You gonna' let these women scare
          you off?

James turns back to the sisters.

                    JAMES WHITAKER (cont'd)
          You should know that you can't win
          against the government. You're
          wasting your time. I'll be back
          tomorrow with the sheriff and some
          workers with a backbone. Have a
          nice night ladies.

James walks away. Lena calls after him.

                    LENA
          You said you were going to move the
          bodies to Quindaro Cemetery.

James turns.

                    JAMES WHITAKER
          Yep.

                    LENA
          What plans do you have for their
          spirits?

Whitaker stares for a moment, but does not answer. He turns and walks away, shaking his head. Lena turns, but Lyda is gone. Lena looks across the cemetery, broken headstones and tall, green grass in all directions.

Lyda is standing in front of several markers, her head hung low. Lena walks up behind her and looks down on the markers. Little Bird Zane on one marker. Sarah Conley on another.

                    LENA(cont'd)
          They have missed you.

Lyda wipes away a tear as she turns to face Lena.

                    LYDA
          How did you know?

                    LENA
          I am Floating Voice.

Lyda turns and looks down at the grave markers for a silent
moment and then turns back to Lena, fire in her eyes.

                    LYDA
          We have to be here before dawn.

                    LENA
          The boats don't run until daybreak.

INT. TELEGRAPH OFFICE - LATER

IDA CONLEY, two long braids framing her face works along with
other telegraph operators closing up for the day,
repositioning papers and photos of loved ones on their desk.
A YOUNG MESSENGER bangs on the front door glass.

Rolling her eyes, Ida looks at the clock.

                    IDA
          We're closed.

Ida turns. The Young Messenger bangs harder.

                    YOUNG MESSENGER
          I know that Ida... This is News!
          You have to get this out now.

Ida opens the door and the Young Messenger runs across the
room and sits down at Ida's desk. Ida slowly sets herself up.
The messenger begins to read. Ida punches out the message.

                    YOUNG MESSENGER(cont'd)
          Mr. Anderson, St. Louis Gazette.
          Stop. Today, July 25, 1906 Huron
          Cemetery Kansas City, Kansas taken
          over. Stop. Government agents
          attempting to gain entry yesterday
          were confronted by two sisters
          whose family are buried there.
          Stop. The sisters say they will not
          leave. Stop. End of message.

Ida types in the last words then stares at the messenger.

EXT. 1842 INDIAN LONGHOUSE - DAWN

The faint light of dawn bathes the village. Smoke from the longhouses lingers just above the trees and Little Bird's breath crystallizes in the cool morning air. Slowly she moves her eyes across the village and beyond. Dark rich greens of the deep grass that stretches before her yield to scattered pines, and then towering oak trees standing on the horizon.

> FLOATING VOICE (V.O.)
> Little Bird saw everything as if it were the last time her eyes would gaze upon the beauty that they were.

She drops her eyes from the vastness as several Indian Chiefs dressed in deerskin enter a low slung log building from different directions. A moment later three men in suits, a fourth carrying a stack of documents, walk from the woods and removing their hats, enter the building.

> FLOATING VOICE (V.O.) (cont'd)
> She had always awoken first, believing the time between darkness and light a gift to be treasured. What happened that day would forever change those moments as the first of many white men invaded her life.

The sun breaks the horizon and the birds begin to sing. LASALLE ARMSTRONG, twenties, tall, dark, with shoulder length black hair steps from the trees and placing his hands over Little Bird's eyes, presses his body against her. She leans her body back against his. He places his lips at her ear.

> LASALLE
> Ti tayatraha yandawaye.
> **(Join me at the river.)**

LaSalle releases his hands and disappears into the woods as Little Bird gives chase.

EXT. WOODS/RIVER - DAY

Little Bird runs through the woods, jumping over fallen logs and ducking under low slung branches. Soft ferns carpet her feet as she runs. A doe hides behind a bush and a hawk lifts from the trees. She comes to a clearing just before the river and sees LaSalle standing on a rock at the water's edge.

With a smile, LaSalle wades into the water. Little Bird waits a moment and then turns her back to him.

LaSalle turns to Little Bird and starts to call out, stops, and slowly makes his way back, taking Little Bird's hand and leading her to sit in the sun. Golden hued leaves float past as they stare at the river.

                    LASALLE
          Yennonhwe kh'ondaon.
          (I love this place.)

                    LITTLE BIRD
          Kiannonhwe. Taoten kh'isen chia
          hatindakion onywandatawan wa
          hatingiadaon?
          **(We both do. But why do you speak
          of that when strange men have
          entered our village?)**

                    LASALLE
          Onhwati ayerihwateri sti stan te
          yondoton. Ayondoton sti d'
          ewentaion os'tore dinde stan te
          chiachrondi.
          **(I've known something for some time
          that I've kept from you. I should
          not have, as the day fast
          approaches and you are not ready.)**

                    LITTLE BIRD
          Taoten ondaie âyechronnist?
          (Ready for what?)

                    LASALLE
          Ayisten dinde wa hatiywannen
          hontendinnon onyiondechawan. Thora
          entawan ekwet chiatrahenk.
          **(My father and the other Chiefs
          have sold our land. In a few days
          we move west.)**

                    LITTLE BIRD
          Stan te yerihwatendi.
          Chawanonronnon dinde Hondasayannen
          henditron awcti ondechaen
          chiatrahenk.
          **(I don't understand. The Shawnee
          and Delaware live on all the land
          west of ours.)**

                    LASALLE
          Haekwendayerati hatendinnonchrondi
          sonywaraskwati onyiondechrawan
          dinde ehaekwatrandey Chawanonronnon
          dinde Hondasayannen.
                         (MORE)

LASALLE (cont'd)
Haonye etikwaion chia ehaekwatendinnon Chawanonronnon wich iwasen ahtere iskare skangwat acres.
(They made a deal for us to leave our land and join the other tribes. Once we arrive, we are to purchase fifty-eight thousand acres from the Shawnee.)

LITTLE BIRD
Acres?
(Acres?)

LASALLE
Ondaie hennondechriati hatinnionyenhak.
(It is the way they divide the land.)

LITTLE BIRD
Aonyi te aiondechrate haekwendayerati hondechrawan kwatrake ekentron Wendat.
(Isn't there enough land for the government east of the Wyandot?)

LASALLE
Ason âhondechraehwandik de haekwendayerati.
(There is never enough land for them.)

LITTLE BIRD
Annen haonye sarihwateri?
(How long have you known?)

LASALLE
Haonye yannendaye.
(Since the frost began to bend the grass.)

LITTLE BIRD
Taot chi te skerihwandoton?
(Why not tell me sooner?)

LASALLE
Ayisten ahayerihwandoton orihwaseti. Te utoyehti de ayonrihwandoton.
(My father trusted me with the plans for the tribe. I couldn't take the chance of telling you.)

Little Bird pulls away from LaSalle and stands.

                    LITTLE BIRD
Te utoyehti de skerihwandoton. Utoyehti kwatatro,en chi onywandiayi. Te utoyehti skerihwandoton âyaraskwa yondaon.
(Take the chance of telling me what? That you trust me enough to make love with you before we are known as one, yet you could not find a reason to tell me I must leave my home.)

LaSalle rises and steps toward Little Bird. She stiffens.

                    LASALLE
Yeywannen eyenk. Ayatrihwaienst yarihwaseti.
(Little Bird. I will be Chief one day and must learn to keep a confidence.)

                    LITTLE BIRD
Steniestha te enri de Wendat!
(Chief of what? Nothing will be left of the Wyandot.)

Little Bird turns and walks off.

EXT. 1907 WYANDOT CEMETERY - EARLY MORNING

Made with non-matching discarded wood an open glassless window, a six foot by eight foot shack has taken form.

A crowd starts to surround the shack as Lyda, perched on the roof, drives a few extra nails into the wooden planks.

Ida approaches, a CORN COB PIPE dangling from her mouth. Smoke billows around her as she makes her way through the crowd. Busting through she stands defiantly a few feet away from the shack.

                    IDA
What is this?

Lena steps outside and Lyda stops hammering.

                    LENA
Lyda, look our big Sister has come to help.

                    IDA
          Answer my question. What is this?

                    LYDA
          It's Fort Conley.

                    IDA
          So I hear. And by now all of
          Missouri and Kansas will have heard
          as well. I expect this type of
          behavior from you, Lena. But Lyda
          what are you doing? You're a
          lawyer.

The crowd begins to back away from Ida as Lyda climbs down, hammer in hand she gets closer to Ida. Lena's by the door.

                    LYDA
          I'm a Wyandot. Just as you are.

Lyda sweeps her hammer across the cemetery.

                    LYDA (cont'd)
          Doctors, farmers, traders, mothers,
          daughters, sons and fathers.
          Methodists and not. What we all are
          is Wyandot.

                    IDA
          I'm not questioning our blood, I'm
          questioning your method. There are
          other ways to handle this.

Lena steps forward.

                    LENA
          No there isn't. What problem is it
          for the government to take a spit
          of land like this? Dead people
          can't fight back. Ida, this is the
          only thing they're going to
          understand.

                    IDA
          Well I don't.

Ida storms off and the crowd begins to thin out.

EXT. WYANDOT CEMETERY - LATER

Lyda and Lena stand outside the front door watching as James Whitaker, SHERIFF LEWISTON, sixty with a full beard and a pot belly as well as several deputies and twenty men with shovels and pick-axes walk toward them.

                  LENA
    We've been expecting you.

                JAMES WHITAKER
    I believe these women are
    trespassing. I want them removed.

Sheriff Lewiston steps up to James.

                SHERIFF LEWISTON
    I've seen her in court Mr.
    Whitaker. She's a lawyer.

                JAMES WHITAKER
    She may be a lawyer, but she's not
    above the law. Remove them.

                LYDA
    The Treaty of Eighteen Eighty-Five
    protects this land. It belongs to
    the Wyandot Tribe. We're not
    trespassing, you are.

James turns to Sheriff Lewiston standing to the side.

                JAMES WHITAKER
    Do something about this.

                SHERIFF LEWISTON
    I'm not sure I can.

                JAMES WHITAKER
    Let's go men, get to work.

The twenty workers follow James. The sisters follow and stand next to the men as they prepare to dig up the headstones and plaques resting in the ground. One large worker raises his pick-axe. He's about to drive it into the ground when Lyda throws herself at his feet. He stops his downward movement a second before impaling Lyda in the chest.

                BIG CONSTRUCTION WORKER
    Damnit!

The Construction Worker walks off.

                    BIG CONSTRUCTION WORKER (cont'd)
            I came here to work, not to kill
            anybody.

James, furious, walks past the worker, grabs the pick-axe from his hand and steps toward a headstone. Lena moves to the side and as he raises his axe she lays down beside the headstone that reads Little Bird Zane, her penetrating eyes never blinking.

                    LENA
            Mr. Whitaker you're welcome to
            spend the day trying to kill me.

Whitaker slowly lowers his pick-axe.

Whitaker walks off, followed by the Construction Workers. Seeing movement above these men, Lyda looks up at the senators office building where on the top floor, a dark figure steps away from the window.

EXT. 1842 WYANDOT VILLAGE - MORNING

Little Bird walks into the village. Her father, STANDING BEAR ZANE, long silver hair braided down his back and an eagle feather tucked behind his ear, waves to his daughter. Without a word he points back toward the longhouse. Little Bird nods and walks toward the entrance.

INT. LONGHOUSE - CONTINUOUS

It's empty except for a single figure huddled against a back wall. RIVER SONG, hair uncombed, her eyes red and swollen sits silently, her eyes fixed on the door. Little Bird sits beside her and places her arm around her mother.

                    LITTLE BIRD
            Yonnionrentendi chientondi.
            (I know your sadness.)

River Song remains motionless.

                    RIVER SONG
            Yonnionrentendi chientondi.
            (He could not have told you.)

                    LITTLE BIRD
            Hayerihwandoton.
            (He did.)

RIVER SONG
Stan te harihwateri.
(He does not know.)

LITTLE BIRD
Annen-en ti tayiyandra. Hoisten horihwandoton aweti yarihwateri.
(Mother, look at me! His father told him all there is to know.)

RIVER SONG
Ara harihwateri d'honarihwandoton.
(He knows only what they tell him.)

LITTLE BIRD
Taot chiarihwateri?
(How do you know this?)

RIVER SONG
Ara yatrihote de yatoyen.
(I listen to the truth.)

LITTLE BIRD
Lasalle, ihawen hatiywannen ehonatitendinnon Chawanonronnon atonronton "acres"
(LaSalle said the Chiefs have agreed to buy many acres from the Shawnee.)

RIVER SONG
Hatiywannen wahia hatirati honterendi achietek yehen dinde hontendinnon achietek eyenk.
(The Chiefs, all six as counted, have forgotten the past and sold our future.)

Tears form in her mother's eyes and roll down her cheeks. Little Bird reaches up and wipes the tears away. Her mother closes her eyes, she reopens them fixed on Little Bird.

RIVER SONG (cont'd)
Ayiena.
(My Little Bird.)

River Song pulls Little Bird to her chest. Little Bird resists.

LITTLE BIRD
Taot hatiywannen hesarihwandoton?
(What have the elders told you?)

                    RIVER SONG
          Steniestha te honyerihwandoton.
          Âkwarihwaen sachiota. Onne haonye
          echiarihwateri.
          **(They have told me nothing. We must
          speak of your grandmother and then
          you will understand.)**

                    LITTLE BIRD
          Kwaweyinnen onywetinnen. Tioskenia
          onywentawandi. Aweti yerihwateri
          de ondaie yarihwateri.
          **(I walked with her. I slept beside
          her. I know all there is to know
          about her.)**

Little Bird pulls her knees to her chest and wraps her arms
around her legs. River Song smiles.

                    RIVER SONG
          Sarihwateri i? Yaro akien.
          Sachiota yangwenienhaon de yandawa,
          dinde onnontutonnion dinde de
          yaronhiate. Ayawen te atatinnen.
          Âyawen yahiatonnen dinde te
          yawendaennen. Sandiyonratoyennen
          i?
          **(Did you know she sat as you do
          now? She did. Your grandmother
          carried with her the blood of the
          river, and of the mountains and of
          the sky. They say that she could
          not speak. That she made marks, but
          words never passed her lips. You
          believe this to be true?)**

                    LITTLE BIRD
          Aa-o. Ehierandi de te atatinnen.
          (Yes, I remember her silence.)

                    RIVER SONG
          Sachiota etsak thora atatinnen.
          Ara yatrihote. Ondwen
          aochiennannont dinde chi ondwen
          aochiennannont dinde chi
          aochiennannont. Onne onhwa
          ayonchiennannont. Ehechiennannont
          chiena dinde eochiennannont oen.
          Te saatendi te chiena,
          eyewendichiay. Eyontahkwi. Yaatsi
          Yawendayra. Echiewendayehte de
          onywen dinde chiena eyachiendayehte
          de skwen, awentenhaon, haonye
          steniestha te awen.
                         (MORE)

                    RIVER SONG (cont'd)
               (Your grandmother spoke often but
               only I could hear her. She had a
               name given to her by her mother and
               her mother before and her mother
               before and now I give it to you.
               And in time you will give it to
               your daughter and she in turn to
               hers. And if there is no daughter,
               one will come seeking the voice. It
               is everlasting... It is "Floating
               Voice". You will be the bearer of
               the words we speak and your
               daughter the bearer of yours until
               there is nothing left to say.)

River Song takes Little Bird's hand.

                    RIVER SONG (cont'd)
               Chiawasti dinde endiyonraenskon,
               ayiena. Haonye âchiaraskwa
               yawitsonnha. Âchiaton onnhetien
               dinde yandiayi. Âchiakonten
               yahwatsirase, chiahwatsirawan.
               Yatonnhara sti yendionraen
               chionnhase. Iohti ochrate awaton
               ya,enrate. Iohti ondientawan
               ondekwannonten yatsistutonnion.
               (You are a beautiful and thoughtful
               child, a daughter like no other. It
               is time for you to leave the
               girlhood thoughts behind, become a
               woman, marry, and begin a new
               family of your own. I feel joy when
               I think of the life that awaits
               you. It is why the seasons change,
               and the snow melts to feed the
               wildflowers. It is your time.)

River Song begins to stroke her daughter's hair and Little
Bird is silenced in the moment.

Little Bird turns to her mother.

                    LITTLE BIRD
               Itha orahwiye haonye yewe chia
               chiawayi yariuta.
               (This morning when I awoke you held
               tightly to a stone.)

                    RIVER SONG
               Okontakwi Yawendayra ayatati chia
               yendawotrahwinnen. Aweskak awen,
               yeriutawan dinde ason yeriutayehte.
                         (MORE)

RIVER SONG (cont'd)
Kha yondaon okontakwi yachitawan
yondechrisen. Eyondechrehwaha
iohti eyonatehwaha de onywariskon.
Kha yariuta ayehiera de tendi.
Yendiyonraen te ayihey haonye
asontaye dinde yewan, ayoki
aiayenhaon aiendera.
(The first time Floating Voice spoke to me, I was walking along the river bed. When she was done speaking, I bent and picked up that stone and I've not let it go. This has been my home since my feet first touched the earth and I will miss it as much as I will miss those that walked here with me. The stone reminds me of them both. I thought that if I died in the night and held tight, the spirits would let me keep it.)

EXT. WYANDOT VILLAGE - NIGHT

Drums beat out in unison as LaSalle and Little Bird, her hair flowing with flowers, begin to dance with the other tribe members around a roaring fire.

To the side, watching with pride, are Little Birds parents.

STANDING BEAR
Chiehiera asontaye haonye
aonywandiaka i?
(Do you remember our wedding night?)

RIVER SONG
(laughing)
Stan te yehiera d'yandrawan.
(If you mean the dancing, no.)

Standing Bear smiles, and placing his arms around River Song pulls her close and whispers in her ear.

STANDING BEAR
Eonywandiyonrawastak, tiena.
(She will make us proud, our Little Bird.)

RIVER SONG
Onywandiyonrawasti.
(She already has.)

                    STANDING BEAR
          Achietek âtennonhwiha. Te tierhe
          onxiatontion. Ennon etichien.
          **(Tomorrow we must get a start on
          the young ones. We don't want to be
          left behind. Let's leave the
          celebrating to others.)**

River Song steps out of Standing Bear's arms to face him.

                    RIVER SONG
          Onywannianni akwarit.
          Etsungiandika yachien. Eyarakieye
          iyerhe yarendut dinde yandrawan
          dinde yachiensti d' onnhase tiena.
          **(There will be time to pack, but
          little time to celebrate. Tonight I
          want to sing and dance and
          celebrate our daughter's new life.)**

River Song extends her hand and Standing Bear takes it with a
smile. Together they dance their way into the crowd. Little
Bird stops for a moment and watches as her mother and father
dance, the embers from the fire swirling around them, the
drum beats matching their movements.

INT. EXPANSIVE ARMY TENT - DAY

The government men in suits are sitting at a table when
GOVERNOR SHANNON of Ohio, late fifties, rotund and balding
arrives with his entourage. The GOVERNOR'S ASSISTANT, a young
man with glasses, steps forward and turns a large book around
so he can read the document enclosed.

                    GOVERNOR'S ASSISTANT
          It reads as we've prepared it.

                    GOVERNOR SHANNON
          Then execute it at once.

The suited men begin to sign as the Governor turns and walks
to the entrance of the tent. He pulls the canvas back and
Wyandot Indians pass before him.

                    GOVERNOR SHANNON (cont'd)
          These people are the worst business
          men alive. Half the state of Ohio
          for less than it costs to build a
          club car. Unimaginable.

The Governor turns and walks back to the table. Leaning down,
he takes a pen and signs his name. A shadow crosses the page.

The Governor turns to see Chief Armstrong and CHIEF SQUIRE
GREY EYES standing behind him. LaSalle is behind his father.

				GOVERNOR SHANNON (cont'd)
			Which one of you speaks English?

No one moves. Chief Armstrong steps aside for LaSalle.

				GOVERNOR SHANNON (cont'd)
			It's okay son.

LaSalle steps forward, staring at the Governor.

				GOVERNOR SHANNON (cont'd)
			You understand me?

The Governor extends a rolled piece of paper. LaSalle looks
at his father.

				GOVERNOR SHANNON (cont'd)
			Take this. You got a good deal from
			The Shawnee.

LaSalle takes the paper and hands it to his father.

The other chiefs have taken seats at the table.

Chief Armstrong joins them as the book is placed before him.

One of the government agents places a pen in the center of
the book. The Chief looks at the others who have signed, one
by one they lower their eyes. The Chief turns the pen to see
the words engraved into the handle. It reads;"Property of
Western Railroad Company."

				CHIEF ARMSTRONG
			Ihatiroch yarontutonnion.
			Ihatieratha âyahiatonchronnia.
			Haonye hatihiaton hotiwendayon.
			**(They cut down trees to make paper
			and then write their empty words.)**

He senses something and opens the scroll given by LaSalle.
It's a MAP to their new land by the RIVER OFF THE HILL.

INT. 1907 SENATORS OFFICE BUILDING - EARLY EVENING

SENATOR CHARLES CURTIS, fifty, sophisticated, dressed in a
business suit sits behind an intricately carved mahogany
desk. On the matching credenza rests a Remington sculpture
and a vase of fresh flowers. Charles never takes his eyes
from the Wayandot.

                    HAROLD (O.S.)
                (Clears throat)
            Uhm...Uhm. Sir?

HAROLD, an assistant shifts in an arm chair across the desk.

                    CHARLES CURTIS
            What is it Harold?

                    HAROLD
            I don't think we've finished our
            meeting.

                    CHARLES CURTIS
            I see.

                    HAROLD
            Mr. Curtis, can I make an
            observation?

Charles never moves his eyes from the window.

                    CHARLES CURTIS
            Yes Harold?

                    HAROLD
            Senator, frankly, you've been,
            ah... distracted. Is there
            something wrong?

                    CHARLES CURTIS
            Stand up!

Harold stands in shock at the tone of demand.

                    CHARLES CURTIS (cont'd)
            Now come over here.

Harold slowly walks over to stand by Charles. Charles points toward Fort Conley.

                    CHARLES CURTIS (cont'd)
            What is that?

                    HAROLD
            It's two crazy Indian sisters...

                    CHARLES CURTIS
            Indians?

                    HAROLD
            No! That's not it. I mean yes...
            but no... I mean.

CHARLES CURTIS
I know what you mean. Our meeting is over.

Harold walks out and silently closes the door. Charles resumes his view of the cemetary below.

INT. FORT CONLEY - CONTINUOUS

Lyda stands in the doorway as Lena lays a blanket across the dirt floor, sits and takes a bite out of an apple.

LENA
Lyda.

LYDA
Yes.

LENA
Would you run me a bath...

Lyda turns, drops next to her sister on the blanket and they roll around together laughing hysterically.

EXT. KANSAS CITY STREETS - DAY

James Whitaker and HORACE B. DURANT, sixty, walk along the streets of Kansas City.

JAMES WHITAKER
It's your problem, Horace.

H.B. DURANT
Calm down, I'm going to take care of it.

JAMES WHITAKER
You better, 'cause no one is going to buy it with those Indian half-breeds living there.

H.B. DURANT
Don't forget that you have to get this done soon. Your commission from the government to move these bodies has an end.

The two men take a sharp turn and begin walking up the hill toward the crest of the cemetery.

EXT. HURON CEMETARY - DAY

They come to the top of the hill and are just twenty yards from Fort Conley. Lena opens the door and steps outside.

          H.B. DURANT
Miss Conley?

          LENA
I'm Lena Conley.

          H.B. DURANT
Miss Conley, my name is Horace B. Durant and I'm the Indian Commissioner. I'm here to discuss your occupation of this property.

          LENA
I can imagine what you mean by Occupation. But I am wondering what exactly is an Indian Commissioner?

          H.B. DURANT
I'm in charge of the relationship between the Indian Tribes and the citizens of the United States.

          LENA
The relationship?

          H.B. DURANT
I'm here to ask you to leave this property.

          LENA
If you would excuse me for a moment I'd like to ask my parents what they think.

          H.B. DURANT
Okay...sure.

Lena goes back into Fort Conley.

          JAMES WHITAKER
There's no one in there.

Lena returns and steps up to H.B Durant.

          LENA
They said you'll have to come back tomorrow.

Lena turns and goes back inside.

JAMES WHITAKER
What the heck was that?

H.B. DURANT
I guess I'll come back tomorrow...

JAMES WHITAKER
You need to take care of this today! Look over there.

Whitaker points to a pile of wire and sticks.

JAMES WHITAKER (cont'd)
That's a fence. I don't want it up.

H.B. DURANT
Don't you do anything foolish, James. I'll come back tomorrow and deal with this. I want to be a little better prepared.

JAMES WHITAKER
These sisters are gonna' be the death of me.

H.B. DURANT
That may be true, just don't count on being buried here.

EXT. 1842 WYANDOT VILLAGE - MORNING

The entire Wyandot Tribe, six hundred thirty-four strong, have gathered in the village center. A platform has been built and SQUIRE GREY EYES steps to the front.

SQUIRE GREY EYES
Etsungiandika eonywaraskwa. Ara thora yawendaye âyihon. Onywaweti onywaronhwannionhonk iohti okwati. Ondaie d'ayoatontion ayotawi iohti yenheon. Ondiri kwatrendaent onnhontion. Saywatrendaensti de Hawendio hatiyondaskehen ayosayi.
(My people, the time for our departure is at hand. A few words remain only to be said. Our entire nation once moved about like the wind. Those that remain, sleep the sleep of death, but the hope of immortality is strong within our breasts. We have committed to the Great Spirit, the grave of our ancestors.)

EXT. WYANDOT VILLAGE - CONTINUOUS

LaSalle steps beside Little Bird and slips his arm around her pulling her close.

> SQUIRE GREY EYES (O.C.)
> Etaenton dinde yarhutonnion Sanduske ason te tsistawen de yarendutonnion dinde saywachiendaenton d'hawendio. Ara aywatsataion.
> **(No more shall Sandusky's Plains and forests echo to the voice of song and praise. It remains only for us to say farewell.)**

EXT. WYANDOT VILLAGE - CONTINUOUS

Governor Shannon steps to the stage, the government men cheer. He attempts to speak in Wyandot.

> GOVERNOR SHANNON
> (clearing his throat)
> Kwe kwatakhen yatonnhara d' skwaraskwan. Yatonnhara skwandatase. Yatonnhara……
> **(Hello, my brothers, I rejoice at your leaving. I rejoice at your new village. I rejoice at... Ah hell.)**

The Governor gives up his attempt.

> GOVERNOR SHANNON (cont'd)
> Okay you know what. Thanks for this friendly visit and I wish you and your people peace, prosperity...

> SUMMUNDUWATT (O.S.)
> Ara handichiaywannen, handichiaywannen
> **(Nothing but lies! Lies! Lies!)**

SUMMUNDUWATT, an elder has tied himself to a tree just a hundred feet from the stage.

> GOVERNOR SHANNON
> Silence him!

Federal Marshals run toward Summunduwatt. LaSalle and Little Bird begin pushing their way through the crowd toward Summunduwatt.

Federal Marshals reach Summunduwatt and try to untie him. Little Bird is the first to reach his side and grabs at the Marshals, who knock her to the ground.

                    GOVERNOR SHANNON (cont'd)
          (screaming)
I want this stopped. I can't have any problems today. I want a peaceful exit!

Summunduwatt spits out his words.

                    SUMMUNDUWATT
Kha ayondaon. Stan te kese.
(This is my home. I will not go!)

                    FEDERAL MARSHAL #1
You have to go.

                    SUMMUNDUWATT
Te kese.
(I will not.)

                    FEDERAL MARSHAL #2
Then we're going to carry you out.
     (to the other Federal
      Marshall)
Get him untied!

They pull on the front ropes and then move to the back of the tree but still can't find the knot.

                    FEDERAL MARSHAL #1
I can't find the knot!

                    FEDERAL MARSHAL #2
Cut it!

Federal Marshal #1 pats himself for a knife.

                FEDERAL MARSHAL #2 (CONT'D) (cont'd)
Move away.

Federal Marshal #2 releases a knife from his belt and steps toward Summunduwatt. The Marshal stands to the side and reaches across Summunduwatt to cut the rope. Summunduwatt, lowers his head and drives his teeth deep into the Marshal's forearm.

                FEDERAL MARSHAL #2 (CONT'D) (cont'd)
Agh...You no good, stupid, red, bastard!

The Marshal steps back and looks down at his bleeding arm. He then plunges the knife into Summunduwatt's heart. The old man grunts with the impact of the knife and as blood runs from the corner of his mouth, he speaks.

                    SUMMUNDUWATT
    Xa iatonnia. Xa eyihej.
    (Here I was born and here I will
    die.)

The Marshal pulls the knife out but before he can thrust it back into Summunduwatt. LaSalle grabs the Marshal by the neck and is about to snap it when he sees Summunduwatt close his eyes and die. Little Bird, her face bruised and dirty crawls toward Summunduwatt.

LaSalle opens his arm and the Marshal drops to his knees gasping for air. LaSalle squeezes the Marshal's arm and the Marshal drops the knife to the ground as he screams in pain. LaSalle takes the knife and stands, towering over the Marshal. The other Marshals draw their guns and point them toward LaSalle. LaSalle turns as Summunduwatt, his head to the side, lays dead in the ropes.

LaSalle helps Little Bird to her feet. She reaches behind Summunduwatt, and taking his hands from behind his back, pulls them into view. Locked inside the old man's hands are the ends of the rope. There were no knots, the elder had simply wrapped himself around the tree and held the ropes behind his back. The ropes fall away and Summunduwatt collapses into LaSalle's arms.

Little Bird turns toward the stunned tribe members and then forcefully takes a blanket from one of them. She places the blanket over Summunduwatt and then LaSalle lifts his body and begins to walk through the village. As he passes the Wyandot, they lower their heads in respect.

INT. GOVERNMENT TENT - LATER

The six chiefs and several government representatives are seated at a long desk in the tent. LaSalle is escorted inside handcuffed. A GOVERNMENT MAN stands and motions for the handcuffs to be released.

                    LASALLE
    I...

Chief Armstrong silences his son with the hand.

                  GOVERNMENT MAN
    You are fortunate that the Governor
    has agreed with your chiefs.
                    (MORE)

                    GOVERNMENT MAN (cont'd)
            You are free to join the others in
            your new home. Go now and be quick
            about it.

The chiefs rise and exit the tent, Chief Armstrong taking
LaSalle by the arm and escorting him from the room.

                    LASALLE
            âhatrio
            (I should have killed him.)

                    CHIEF ARMSTRONG
            âchienhej.
            (And you would be as dead as he.)

Chief Armstrong walks away leaving LaSalle silenced.

EXT. 1908 FORT CONLEY - EARLY EVENING

Lena and Lyda are completing the fence around Fort Conley.
Shadows are giving way to the setting sun as a group of
children play in the cemetery. A few of the children begin
playing leapfrog over the headstones. Seeing this, Lena picks
up a stick and starts marching toward the children.

                    LENA
            Move on! All of you out!

The children, at first frozen in fear, gather their senses
and begin to run.

                    LENA (cont'd)
            You two over there, wait.

SHERMAN HARDING and his younger sister ANN GARRETT HARDING
stop and turn around. Lena lowers her stick and approaches
the children.

                    LENA (cont'd)
            You're Wyandot.

The children nod their heads.

                    LENA (cont'd)
            Then this is your place too. Come,
            I want to show you something.

Lena starts to walk off but the children remain.

                    LENA (cont'd)
            Come on. It's okay.

The children slowly follow Lena. They stop beside her as she kneels beside a plaque set in the ground. The bronze and stone marker is buried in the deep grass. Lena runs her hand over the marker, pulling back the grass to reveal the writing. "Unknown Child, Survey 1896 - James Whitaker".

                    LENA (cont'd)
    To James Whitaker the child was
    unknown.

Lena places her hand back on the plaque.

                    LENA (cont'd)
    This child had a name, Mattootook.
    He was born and died in a single
    day. This is the only home he's
    ever known.

The children, wide-eyed, step back. Lena smiles as she gets to her feet.

                    LENA (cont'd)
    He said he enjoyed the game today.

Ann starts to giggle and Sherman smiles. Lena, followed by the children, walks to another part of the cemetery and stops at what seems to be an unmarked area.

                    LENA (cont'd)
    Marked or unmarked, this place is
    alive with the spirits of our
    ancestors.

Lena removes a deerskin pouch from her dress pocket and opening it, takes out a handful of tobacco.

                    LENA (cont'd)
    Do you know how to pray?

                ANN GARRETT HARDING
    I do.

                        LENA
    Do you know how to pray to the sky?
    To the river? To the rocks?

The children shake their heads no.

                    LENA (cont'd)
    Put out your hands.

Tentatively the children put out their hands and Lena places a small amount of tobacco in each.

LENA (cont'd)
Now hold this. I want to teach you to pray.

Lena crouches down to the children's level.

LENA (cont'd)
Listen repeat what I say. Yaronhiate.
(Sky).

ANN AND SHERMAN
Yaronhiate.
(Sky)

LENA
Onne.
(Behold)

ANN AND SHERMAN
Onne.
(Behold)

LENA
Ayonstaenkhwas.
(Offer thee in sacrifice)

ANN AND SHERMAN
Ayonstaenkhwas
(Offer thee in sacrifice)

LENA
Tayitenr.
(Have pity on me, assist me)

ANN AND SHERMAN
Tayitenr
(Have pity on me, assist me)

LENA
Now, throw your tobacco and say it with me.

The children and Lena throw their tobacco into the air.

ANN, SHERMAN AND LENA
Yaronhiate onne ayonstaenkhwas tayitenr.Tayitenr
(Oh, Sky, here is what I offer thee in sacrifice; have pity on me, assist me.)

INT. FORT CONLEY - NIGHT

Two mats are rolled and placed in the corner. A small table with a few books sits on the side and Lyda, barefoot, is writing by candlelight. There is a knock and Ida enters.

LYDA
This is a surprise.

IDA
I was told there were more visitors from the government.

Ida looks around the Fort.

LYDA
I've been working on a brief. I think it's time to file a motion to protect the cemetery. Lena's nasty demeanor will only hold the sheriff off so long.

IDA
Don't you think the fort has served its purpose? You stopped them from taking the grave markers.

Lyda turns back to her papers and begins writing again.

IDA (cont'd)
When does it end? It's okay for you and Lena. I'm the one that has to work with people who don't really understand what you're doing up here. They think the Conley sisters are crazy. Remember, I'm your sister.

LYDA
If it stops them, they can think I'm as crazy as a loon.

IDA
This must end. I need you and Lena to come back home.

LYDA
We are home.

IDA
It's not the same.

There's a soft knock on the door. REBECCA HARDING, thirty, red hair and black eyes, slips inside with a bag.

                    LYDA
          Welcome, Rebecca.

                    REBECCA HARDING
          I've brought a hot meal - brisket
          and potatoes.

                    LYDA
          Thank you.

                    REBECCA HARDING
          No. Thank you for what you are
          doing. And tell Lena what she did
          with my children was wonderful.

                    LYDA
          We're doing it for all of us.

Rebecca nods her head stepping outside. Ida follows.

                    IDA
          I'll walk with you.

                    REBECCA HARDING
          That would be nice.

Ida and Rebecca step outside and seemingly by instinct Ida
looks down at a marker and smiles. The name Sarah Conley
clearly seen in the moonlight. They begin to walk through the
cemetery toward the street.

                    IDA
          I'm not sure what they're doing is
          a good idea.

                    REBECCA HARDING
          Whitaker would have already moved
          the headstones, and soon enough the
          bones of our parents and their
          parents.

                    IDA
          Have you heard the rumors about us?

                    REBECCA HARDING
          They are spoken by shallow people.
          What your family is doing is a
          thing of honor.

                    IDA
          The honor of being a laughingstock?

Rebecca stops walking. Ida takes a few more steps then turns.

                    REBECCA HARDING
          Ida, listen. Do you hear anyone
          laughing? My father isn't laughing.
          Tall Charles and Moses Peacock
          aren't laughing. And certainly your
          parents aren't laughing.

                    IDA
          How could you understand? It's not
          you they're laughing at.

                    REBECCA HARDING
          I guess the laughter is too loud
          for you to hear the praise of your
          ancestors.

INT. FORT CONLEY - LATE NIGHT

Lyda is still writing. The door opens and Lena, removing her shoes, steps inside. Lena reaches above the door and removes a small box from the rafters. Written across the box are the words "WAR CHEST".

Lena opens the box and reaching into the pocket of her dress, removes a handful of bills and silver coins. She drops the money into the box and places it back in the rafters. The sisters smile at each other. Lyda continues to write and Lena rolls out a mat then lays down and closes her eyes.

EXT. 1842 COUNTRYSIDE - DAY

The Wyandot Tribe, make their way in a caravan of wagons, horses, and on foot across the countryside.

Little Bird has stopped and watches the faces of the others as they walk past her. Young faces smiling, old faces understanding, and far too many faces showing the deep sadness of the move.

The final wagon has passed Little Bird and a few slow moving elders pass without a word spoken. Little Bird stands alone looking back at her village. In the distance, a caravan of settlers is seen stark against the black smoke of the burning longhouses.

                    FLOATING VOICE (V.O.)
          In years past, the smoke that
          spread across the sky would have
          foretold of a great feast, or the
          return of our chief. Today, the
          smoke foretold nothing but pain.
                         (MORE)

                    FLOATING VOICE (V.O.) (cont'd)
          By sunrise tomorrow there would be
          nothing left of the Wyandot home.
          The longhouse ashes would be spread
          amongst the memories. And tomorrow
          in the land that we once called
          home we would surely be forgotten.

EXT. COUNTRYSIDE - NIGHT

As the campfires die away, a few Indians walk around the
sleeping bodies. LaSalle sits alone by a fire. Little Bird
joins him. She places her hand on his shoulder, lets it slide
across his chest and then up to stroke his face.

                    LITTLE BIRD
          Stan te âyendiyonraen, ayonhwa âye.
          Yaro tontase, ekandare
          **(I could not imagine this journey
          without you. Please come back to
          me.)**

                    LASALLE
          Summunduwatt hayahkwan yaraskwan.
          (Summunduwatt won't let me go.)

                    LITTLE BIRD
          Isa, te chierhe. Saton
          chiatontawan. Tiatationnonhwes.
          Summunduwatt ahatiatontawa.
          **(It is you that won't let go. Don't
          waste a moment of your freedom, my
          love. Summunduwatt is free.)**

Little Bird turns LaSalle's face to hers.

Little Bird kisses LaSalle and LaSalle responds.

EXT. COUNTRYSIDE - MONTAGE SEQUENCE

                    FLOATING VOICE (V.O.)
          River Song seemed to know when we
          were reaching the end of our
          Wayandot lands. She walked
          silently, her heart breaking with
          every step. No one noticed the
          touch of her hand on their cheek or
          a kiss given secretly in the night.
          We wrapped her body in a blanket
          and buried her beside the river for
          which she was named.

The sun shines bright across the flattening land. The hills have given way to lowlands and riverbeds running as far as the eye can see.

The caravan presses on in a torrential rain. The leaves starting to turn from green to yellow and orange blow about in a ferocious wind. A wagon gets stuck and it's wheels sink completely into the swollen ground.

The family inside makes their way out and joins the others whose wagons lay like dead carcasses behind the tribe.

Standing Bear walks alone, his head hung low.

Little Bird helping an elder walk in the mud.

Children dying in their parents arms as they walk in the cold morning air.

The leaves are now gone from the trees and the wind whipping across open fields as the caravan continues.

LaSalle at his father's death bed. His father hands him the MAP before he passes away.

Winter storm clouds gather as the diminished tribe stops in an open area. In the distance, is the RIVER OFF THE HILL.

EXT. 1843 WYANDOT KANSAS VILLAGE - THE NEXT MORNING

The sun breaks through the clouds and casts it's light upon the deep snow covered village. Slowly, the Indians emerge and begin to clear areas to start fires. LaSalle and Little Bird step from their cover.

A SHAWNEE CHIEF, leading several fierce Indian warriors on horseback, enters the makeshift village. They stop and look around the camp.

                    SHAWNEE CHIEF
     Annen haywannen.
     (Where is your Chief?)

LaSalle, with Little Bird at his side, steps up to the Shawnee group.

                    SHAWNEE CHIEF (cont'd)
     Haonye ondrahta atiarenta iohti,
     Chawanonronnon te honatitrandi
     hatiywannen de Wendat. Ara atati.
     Te haaywatistakwandi atendinnonchra
     ondecha yaio owhistandoron.
     Aywaehwandi onywondechawan.
                    (MORE)

SHAWNEE CHIEF (cont'd)
Te aywaehwandi owhistandoron skwawhistawan.
(When the leaves were golden, the Shawnee met with the elders of your tribe. They were given only a hope, not a promise of land for money. It has been decided that we need our land more than your money.)

LASALLE
Hennenheon. Etsungiandika ehaaywannontra. Tiondehwandi.
(They are dead and we will soon follow. We need land to survive.)

SHAWNEE CHIEF
Chawanonronnon stan te aywatendinnon tsondechrawan.
(It was not the Shawnee that sold your land.)

LaSalle steps closer to the Shawnee Chief.

LASALLE
Kwiohti chierhe Chawanonronnon skwandiayensenni aientronkwi kwatrake. Ayoskwinnon iohti arakwa yaronhwan de yaronhiate.
(Do you think the Shawnee are safe from those that push from the east? They are moving faster than the sun across the sky.)

Little Bird places her hand on her stomach.

LITTLE BIRD
Chi ekha yachiaahate iwes Chawanonronnon te honatitrandey de Wendat. Tsinnen skwatendinnon tsondechrawan? Kwiohti ewetsinnonstaten? Ara ywenditi ondechra yayont onnhase. Okenie de ywenditi ondechra.
(Before this child walks the Shawnee will join the Wyandot. Who will you seek land from and will they turn you away? We ask for only enough land to begin a new life. It is but a small part of the Shawnee lands.)

SHAWNEE CHIEF
Te yatoyen de sen,
eayiondechrehwanha aweti
onyiondechrawan.
Onyionnhonyannondi.
**(If what you say is true, we will
need all of our land. The decision
has been made.)**

The Shawnee Chief and his warriors turn their horses and begins to ride away.

LASALLE
Atiesen skwaatontion.
(You turn from us with great ease.)

The Chief continues.

LASALLE (cont'd)
Te atiesen stan te
skwakatannenchronhwiche haonye
aiheon ewesti skwachitaye.
Chawanonronnon haywannen hohten
hochiaten. Hatati chia
hakonchiatase.
**(But you will not be able to cover
your eyes from the dead that will
pile at your feet.)**

The Shawnee Chief stops his horse and speaks without turning.

SHAWNEE CHIEF
Sahwen haonye chiena eokwetonde.
(Stay until your child is born.)

LITTLE BIRD
Kha tewenk aweskak d'esk8entesa.
**(This will not happen until the
days begin to lengthen.)**

The Shawnee Chief pulls his horse around.

SHAWNEE CHIEF
Âhechiatones ekha yachiaaha
atunditem.
**(Then you have this child to thank
for your good fortune.)**

The Chief jerks his horse and is off.

LaSalle takes Little Bird by the hand and begins to walk.

INT. 1908 IDA CONLEY FAMILY HOME - DAWN

A pale light illuminates the living room of the Conley home. Paintings and books line the walls, several overstuffed chairs and an ottoman stand in the corners. Pictures of the Conley sisters and their parents sit along a coffee table. Ida sleeps on a sofa, a thin wooden board across her chest.

Startled, Ida awakens and putting the board down, she begins to straighten the pillows on the sofa. As she does she sees the corner of a bible showing under the skirt of the sofa.

Ida bends to pick up the bible and sees there is something written on the inside cover. She quickly lights a candle and discovers written in neat, perfect script, the words:

"First bible of SARAH MCINTYRE CONLEY, first born daughter of Eliza Zane Conley, Wayandot and her husband Andrew S. Conley Fur Trader. Ida slowly lowers the candle to the bottom of the page where beautiful handwritten script spell out Sarah M. Conley and written in large childlike letters just below that is the name IDA.

Ida kisses the page of the bible and places it in a bookcase.

INT. CONLEY FAMILY HOME - MOMENTS LATER

Ida stands at the door, a rolled up carpet, a wooden board and a small suitcase in hand. She looks around the room one last time and then leaves the house.

EXT. FORT CONLEY - MORNING

Ida stands at the gate that Lyda and Lena have built with a a fence around Fort Conley. Ida fastens a wooden board on the gate. Lena steps outside followed by Lyda holding a stack of papers. Their smile disappears as they look past Ida.

Ida turns to see H.B. Durant and James Whitaker, along with two other men in suits, standing a hundred feet away. Ida opens the gate and steps inside with her sisters. As she closes the gate the sign she has placed on the gate reads: "YOU TRESPASS AT YOUR OWN PERIL".

Whitaker begins to walk toward the sisters, who are now unified behind the fence.

                    JAMES WHITAKER
        I told you, Durant! Look at that
        damn fence.

                    H.B. DURANT
          The fence is the least of my
          worries.

Ida begins to unroll the carpet. Inside is a shotgun. Lena
grabs it and Whitaker and Durant stop.

                    JAMES WHITAKER
          I want them gone.

The group of men stop just outside the gate. H.B. Durant
reads the sign and then looks up.

                    H.B. DURANT
          I don't want any trouble.

                    LENA
          Then leave. This I tell you, the
          first man who tries to turn a sod
          of soil over one of these graves
          will first have to turn another for
          themselves.

                    JAMES WHITAKER
          Durant!

                    LYDA
          Durant... I believe you'll find
          your name among these documents.

                    H.B. DURANT
          What documents are those, Miss
          Conley?

                    LYDA
          Your office will get a copy from
          the court. But, since you've taken
          the trouble to come all the way up
          here I'll be happy to tell you.
          This is a petition for injunction
          in the Circuit Court for the
          District of Kansas. As a citizen-
          Wyandot I have a legal estate in
          this cemetery.

                    H.B. DURANT
          I don't claim to be a lawyer,
          however I have two of the finest in
          all of Kansas here with me today.
          Perhaps you'd like to show them
          your documents.

                    LYDA
          They'll read them when you do. Tell
          me Mr. Durant, Article Six of the
          Constitution of the United States
          is still in effect, yes?

                    H.B. DURANT
          To the best of my knowledge Article
          Six, as well as the law that
          authorizes the sale of this
          property, is still valid.

                    LYDA
          If that is the case, then I would
          say I'll sleep very well this
          evening.

                    H.B. DURANT
          I will as well.

                    LYDA
          You have no idea what Article Six
          says, for if you did you wouldn't
          sleep at all, Mr. Durant. You'd be
          on an all-night train to
          Washington. May I remind you that
          it states, "All treaties are the
          supreme law of the land," and sir
          we have a treaty protecting this
          property forever. Good day.

Lyda turns and walks into Fort Conley, followed by Ida. Lena
remains, the shotgun aimed at the two men. Durant walks off.
Whitaker, shocked runs after him followed by the two men.

                    JAMES WHITAKER
              Hold on Durant! That's it?

Whitaker catches Durant and stops him as he starts down the
side of the cemetery toward the street.

                    H.B. DURANT
          This has quickly gotten out of
          hand. It is far beyond my office's
          ability to rectify. I believe this
          is a matter for the Justice
          Department and Federal Marshals.

                    JAMES WHITAKER
          What about the sale?

                    H.B. DURANT
          You might be wise to do as I do.
          Wash your hands of the whole mess.

INT. FORT CONLEY - NIGHT

Inside, the darkness is complete. There is a slap... then another slap. A match is struck and a lantern is lit, illuminating the room. Ida drops back down between her sisters. All three women are wearing soaked nightgowns, the sweat pouring from their bodies.

          IDA
I joined you for this? My God, it must be a hundred and ten in here.

          LENA
Hell couldn't be any hotter.

Lyda's arm flies up as she slaps herself in the forehead. Lena sits up her eyes moving around the room. She stops and stares at Ida.

          LENA (cont'd)
Don't move.

Lena slowly draws her hand back. Ida jumps to her feet.

          IDA
Don't you dare!

Lena lays back down laughing.

          LYDA
I can't sleep like this. This heat is choking me.

          LENA
Then maybe we need to cool off.

          IDA
No...

          LENA
Yes.

EXT. RIVER - MOMENTS LATER

All three sisters are swimming naked in the moon lit river.

          LENA
We haven't done this since we were kids.

          IDA
I've never been naked in this river.

Lyda looks up toward the Bank Building just as the light in the upper office goes dark. She turns and makes a dolphin dive and comes up on her back, her body glistening in the moonlight, her hair flowing around her.

                    LYDA
This is heaven.

                    LENA
Sixty years ago our grandparents swam here. I would have loved to have talked to them.

                    IDA
Little Bird and LaSalle... the stories of their love are told by all the elders.

Lyda drops her legs and the water moves around her shoulders and the three sisters move into a tight circle.

                    LYDA
I wonder who I'll fall in love with. I'm sure no one as great as LaSalle.

                    LENA
Why not. You deserve someone powerful... you need someone powerful.

                    LYDA
What does that mean?

                    IDA
That means you're difficult.

Lyda splashes Ida and a full out water fight ensues.

                  IDA (cont'd)
I'm in love...

On the word "love" the fight stops and Lyda and Lena glide over to within feet of Ida.

                    LYDA
What?

                    IDA
I've fallen in love.

                    LENA
With who?

LYDA
When?

IDA
The last few months...

LYDA
Who is it?

IDA
Nathaniel Davis.

LENA
The fabric store owner?

IDA
Yes.

LENA
No wonder no one knew. Have you been out with him?

IDA
Not yet.

LYDA
Well now... That should tie everything up nicely for the gossip crowd. Between Fort Conley and Ida's black lover we are certain to be the talk of the town for years. Or at least until Lena does something more interesting.

Lena jumps on Lyda's back and tries to push her under. Ida tries to grab Lena off and the three of them wrestle in the waist deep water.

INT. 1843 WYANDOT KANSAS VILLAGE - DAY

Standing Bear is alone in a U.S. Army tent. Relentless rain pelts the tent. A very pregnant, drenched Little Bird enters.

LITTLE BIRD
Kwe, ayisten.
(Hello, Father.)

Standing Bear looks up, with no change in his expression.

STANDING BEAR
Eyatsistetsik Iyerhe akwet oyateye.
(The wildflowers will be high and I long for our walk to the cave.)

LITTLE BIRD
Yarakwa te atiatutandi onnianni.
Ondechate ochiatorendi. Kwiohti
sandiyonratoyen yatsistutonnion.
(The sun has not shown itself for many weeks. Our Mother Earth suffers. Are you sure there are any wildflowers at all?)

STANDING BEAR
Ayeayenhon yatsistutonnion.
Onyehiera.
(I saw them. They wait for me.)

LITTLE BIRD
Ayisten, ennon echie. Ekwet thora
atekaatahton yaro chia kwaonti.
(You can't go Father. We walked for months to get here.)

STANDING BEAR
Etsungiandika ayonhwa tho eyaont.
Tho âyet.
(Without the tribe it will take only weeks and I must go.)

LITTLE BIRD
Ayeyenk de yawiratonnonnion de
yaerati chiendrawan de
hatinnionyen. Esachiendaen,
Haatut Hannionyen. Onhwa
onn'achiateskweten ondiyonhiayi.
(I have seen the scars of your prior dances with bears. You are honored with the great name Standing Bear... you are old now and this is foolish.)

STANDING BEAR
Stan teyese, ondiyonhiayi. Tho
eyet ara yehen.
(Staying away is the foolish deed. I will make the walk one last time.)

Little Bird goes to the door of the tent.

LITTLE BIRD
Etiariskon.
(Then I will join you.)

STANDING BEAR
Chiateihtha dinde sandiyonront
ayien. Ayonhwa tho eyet.
(MORE)

                    STANDING BEAR (cont'd)
          **(You are a brave and thoughtful
          daughter, but I will go alone.)**

                    LITTLE BIRD
          Chiateihtha dinde sandiyont,
          ayisten de eskerihwaiensten.
          Eheyenk Lasalle dinde eyenhawi
          thora ichiesti yaronhwawan.
          **(And you are a brave and thoughtful
          father who taught me. Allow me to
          see LaSalle and gather a few things
          for the trip.)**

INT. U.S. ARMY TENT - MOMENTS LATER

LaSalle sits alone, sharpening a knife. Little Bird enters and a broad smile crosses LaSalle's mouth. He jumps to his feet and covers her with a blanket. LaSalle places his hand on Little Bird's stomach.

                    LASALLE
          Hoskenrayete hario onhwa entate.
          (My warrior is practicing today.)

                    LITTLE BIRD
          Aton onnhetien.
          (Perhaps it is a girl.)

                    LASALLE
          Aonyi te aiaton oskenrayete.
          (And she will not be a warrior?)

                    LITTLE BIRD
          Askennonia oskenrayete ioti
          hachiota..
          **(A peaceful warrior, much as her
          grandfather has been for me.)**

Little Bird takes LaSalle's hand.

                    LITTLE BIRD (cont'd)
          Staqnding Bear onsaret oyateye
          ayiandathareskon. iHerhe onhwa
          the onot. Iyerhe âayiriskon.
          **(Standing Bear is going to return
          to the cave we have visited all our
          lives. He is prepared to go alone,
          but I believe I should go with
          him.)**

                    LASALLE
          Taot iohti sonhwa dinde tiena
          âtsiriskon.
                         (MORE)

LASALLE (cont'd)
(Why would you put yourself and our child in danger?)

LITTLE BIRD
Te yatandihak eyenhatie. Onhwa stan teyatandihe. Eayiriskon sti haonhwa dinde hayiehwandi dinde hiehwandi. Iyerhe âsaraha.
(I have never lived my life in fear and I will not now. I join him because he is alone and needs me, and I need him. I go with your blessing.)

LASALLE
Saehwandi thora hotiskenrayete hatiriskon.
(You will need a handful of warriors to go with you.)

LITTLE BIRD
Haaywaehwandi hotiskenrayete. utoyehti hawaronta dinde yanderi hiariskon.
(It is more dangerous with warriors. No harm will come to an old man and a woman with child.)

LASALLE
Etsungiandika, ayatonnia tiena. Chawanonronnon haywannen ahenhaon âskwaraskwa. Se. Yaroye tontase. Yonehwandi.
(Soon our child will be born and as the Shawnee have said, we must leave. So go, but return quickly as I need you with me.)

Little Bird kisses LaSalle and walks off.

INT. SENATORS OFFICE BUILDING - DAY

Charles sits behind his desk in a heated meeting with James Whitaker and RANDOLPH JOHNSON, tall, silver hair.

JAMES WHITAKER
You either abide by the law or you don't.

CHARLES CURTIS
What law are they breaking?

                    JAMES WHITAKER
          The government wants this land
          sold.

                    CHARLES CURTIS
          Sold to who?

                    JAMES WHITAKER
          I don't care who they sell it to...
          I just want this done with.

                    CHARLES CURTIS
          For someone that doesn't care
          Whitaker you sure are passionate
          about it.

                    JAMES WHITAKER
          I do my job.

Charles stands without warning and Whitaker flinches. Charles
glances at Whitaker and smiling walks over to the window and
looks down.

                    CHARLES CURTIS
          I wish I could stay and watch this
          unfold, but I have to get back to
          Washington. These Conley sisters
          seem to have a plan and I'm not
          sure what you want me to do or even
          if I care to involve myself.

                    JAMES WHITAKER
          You're the senator from Kansas and
          you will be involved if you want to
          or not.

Charles, his temper just under the surface whips his body
around to face Whitaker and speaks through clenched teeth.

                    CHARLES CURTIS
          Careful Whitaker you are entering a
          room without an exit.

                    RANDOLPH JOHNSON
          Interesting. A servant of the
          people comes to ask for your
          assistance with a serious matter
          and you treat him like the
          criminal. I support the decision of
          our great country and came only to
          see what your response might be.
                    (MORE)

                    RANDOLPH JOHNSON (cont'd)
               I expected nothing less and it will
               be the first of your many mistakes
               I will be pleased to present to the
               citizens of Kansas.

                    CHARLES CURTIS
               You think you can buy the senate
               seat Randolph?

Randolph now stands.

                    RANDOLPH JOHNSON
               I know I can.

Johnson walks to the door followed by Whitaker. Whitaker
stops to say something but Charles has moved toward them and
when Whitaker turns, Charles is three feet from him, his eyes
stone cold.

                    CHARLES CURTIS
               Not a single word.

Whitaker backs down in the face of Charles resolve and leaves
the room. Charles remains motionless at the window looking
down at Lyda as she sweeps the ground around Fort Conley. As
he watches, the leaves turn from green to gold and brown and
begin falling from the trees.

EXT. FORT CONLEY - DAY

                    FLOATING VOICE (V.O.)
               As the days past the spirits grew
               as restless as the leaves that
               swirled around the sisters. It was
               their peace they sought and so the
               struggle would continue.

Lyda sweeps the leaves into a pile as it starts to snow. Lyda
stops sweeping and is still for a moment. She then looks up
through the snow at the senators office building. Lyda and
Charles' eyes meet for the first time.

EXT. DISTRICT COURT - DAY

Lyda hunched over to protect her papers leans into the
howling wind and driving snow as she makes her way up the
courthouse stairs.

INT. DISTRICT COURT - DAY

Lyda sits at a table in the front of the courtroom. The United States government has four suited lawyers at the table adjacent to Lyda. The judge, CHARLES BLOOD SMITH, robed and regal, leans forward in his chair. He speaks above the gold letters that spell out his name against the teak wood plaque.

JUDGE CHARLES BLOOD SMITH
District Judge John C. Pollock has asked that I determine and report whether said bill is susceptible of amendment so as to come within the jurisdiction of this court. After reviewing the documents as presented to the Circuit Court for the District of Kansas, it is my finding that the court lacks jurisdiction to proceed in this matter. There is no basis for federal jurisdiction over the complaint. The complaint is dismissed.

The four government lawyers congratulate each other and leave. The judge signs a few papers, gets up from the bench, and walks to the door of his chambers. He stops and looks back at Lyda signing her name to a stack of papers.

JUDGE CHARLES BLOOD SMITH (CONT'D)
(cont'd)
Miss Conley.

LYDA
Yes, Your Honor?

JUDGE CHARLES BLOOD SMITH
You did hear my verdict?

LYDA
Yes I did, Your Honor.

JUDGE CHARLES BLOOD SMITH
Then exactly what are you doing?

Lyda gathers the papers and walks to the Judge.

LYDA
With all due respect, Your Honor, I'm signing my appeal.

Lyda turns and walks out of the courtroom.

INT. TELEGRAPH OFFICE - SAME

Four woman sit behind telegraph machines punching out messages. Their desks are cluttered with family photos and other personal items. The desk next to Ida's is empty.

NANCY, twenty-five another telegraph operator sits down at the empty desk for just a moment. She reaches up and begins taking photographs off the desk and placing them in her purse. Finished she stands and steps over to Ida's desk.

Ida looks up at Nancy who slaps Ida across her face.

> NANCY
> I wish you were dead along with your precious ancestors.

Nancy walks off.

> TELEGRAPH CO. PRESIDENT (O.S.)
> Ida.

Ida turns to see the TELEGRAPH COMPANY PRESIDENT standing outside his office.

> TELEGRAPH CO. PRESIDENT (CONT'D)
> (cont'd)
> I need to see you.

Ida gets up from her desk and touching her cheek, walks into his office. He closes the door and Ida sits down.

> TELEGRAPH CO. PRESIDENT (cont'd)
> I'm sorry to have to do this, but you're employment with our company is terminated.

> IDA
> I don't understand. We're busy.

> TELEGRAPH CO. PRESIDENT
> The government has pulled our contract and that was more than fifty percent of our business. You are the reason for this unfortunate situation. Take any personal belongings and leave at once.

The Telegraph Company President leaves his office and walks directly to the front door and opens it. He stands, waiting for Ida to leave. Ida exits without a word.

INT. LIBRARY - LATER

Lyda sits with books open and writes with a nib pen on a single piece of paper.

          CHARLES CURTIS (O.S.)
  Excuse me, Miss Conley?

Startled and a bit shy, Lyda looks up at the darkly handsome Charles and immediately checks her tortoise shell hair comb.

          CHARLES CURTIS (cont'd)
  I'm sorry if I've disturbed you.

          LYDA
  No, no. I was just doing a little writing.

          CHARLES CURTIS
  I'd say you're doing more than that. You're turning Kansas City on its ear. But I'm sorry, we've not been properly introduced. My name is Charles Curtis, I'm the Sen...

          LYDA
  Sir... I know who you are.

          CHARLES CURTIS
  Do you mind if I sit for a moment?

          LYDA
  Please.

Charles takes his seat.

          CHARLES CURTIS
  I wanted to tell you that I believe what you are doing is courageous and if there is anything you need from me or my office I want you to ask.

          LYDA
  Is it too much to ask that the government leave our ancestors at peace?

          CHARLES CURTIS
  It is not.

          LYDA
  There is evil at work here.

CHARLES CURTIS
Well I expect...

LYDA
When the Wyandots were dying along the river bed and being buried on the high ground no one knew this would be the center of Kansas City. Those that have much want more.

CHARLES CURTIS
I want to continue this conversation but need to get ready for an event tonight. I know this is short notice, but would you be interested in attending a political fund raiser with me this evening.

LYDA
Are you certain?

CHARLES CURTIS
Although it has been from a distance, I've given this a great deal of thought.

LYDA
Then it would be my pleasure to accompany you, however I would appreciate a more formal invitation. You'll need the permission of my eldest sister, Sarah.

CHARLES CURTIS
Where can I find her?

LYDA
She's waiting for you at the top of the hill.

CHARLES CURTIS
The cemetery?

LYDA
Yes.

CHARLES CURTIS
Alright, I'll go right away. And if I'm successful, where can I find you?

LYDA
Not to worry.

Moving quickly, Charles puts on his coat. The collar's up. He moves to the door, opens it and steps outside.

EXT. LIBRARY - DAY

He looks up and sees a large rock jutting out from the hillside above him. Charles blows in his hands and then starts up the slope toward Fort Conley.

EXT. FORT CONLEY - DAY

He gets a few feet from the door and it opens. Lena, scowling, raises the shotgun. Charles throws his hands up.

          CHARLES CURTIS
Hold on now! I mean you no harm. I was sent by your sister Lyda.

          LENA
For what purpose?

          CHARLES CURTIS
Are you Sarah?

          LENA
No.

          CHARLES CURTIS
May I speak with her? Lyda said I should speak to Sarah.

Lena lowers the shotgun and points with her finger to the side of Fort Conley. Charles looks down to his side and sees a grave marker partially covered in snow. It reads SARAH MCINTYRE CONLEY.

Charles looks back up, but Lena has closed the door. Charles kneels in front of the grave and places his hand on the marker. He wipes the snow away to see the dates 1864-1880.

Charles raises his eyes from the grave stone and a hundred spirts stand in the cemetery in front of him. They connect.

He gets to his feet, a confident and determined expression on his face. He turns to find Lyda a few feet away.

          LYDA
She said it would be fine.

EXT. COUNTRYSIDE - DAY

The rain has ceased and a brilliant sun is high in the sky. Little Bird and Standing Bear are walking through a large open area, the grass knee deep.

                  LITTLE BIRD
    Stan tesen sti ahson orahwiye.
    (You haven't said a word all morning.)

                  STANDING BEAR
    Yeatonesenhatie onywandwen sti onywannonten tiariskon.
    (I've been thanking mother for our time together.)

                  LITTLE BIRD
    Aa-o onywariskon. Âyenhwa.
    (Yes...she walks with us. ...The least she could do is carry something.)

Standing Bear laughs as Little Bird smiles. They walk on in silence. They stop and stare to the horizon. The land is marked from East to West with deep wagon tracks. A few old boxes, wagon wheels and rotten food have been discarded.

Beyond the tracks the grass ends in a sea of mud. Chest high posts rest eight feet apart across the horizon. In the distance, a settler and his family erect cross members between the fence posts.

Little Bird turns to her father.

                  LITTLE BIRD (cont'd)
    Ayisten.
    (Oh, Father!)

Standing Bear wraps his arms around her.

EXT. WYANDOT KANSAS VILLAGE - DAY

Water remains puddled around LaSalle who stands with several men from the tribe.

                  TRIBE MEMBER #1
    Asonywastaenkhwas. Âsonywannont ondechase dinde owhistandoron. Onywaehwandi yandiaha dinde yannonchiaennon. steniestha te sonywannont.
    (We were promised land and money.
         (MORE)

                    TRIBE MEMBER #1 (cont'd)
          **We must have food and better
          shelter. We've received nothing.)**

                    LASALLE
          Xa yarihwate yientes.
          (I know this.)

                    TRIBE MEMBER #2
          Tayerihwandoton d'echier.
          **(Then tell me what you're going to
          do?)**

                    LASALLE
          Ahenthaha, haekwendayerati.
          Ahenditha atendacha dinde
          whistandoron. Wa steniestha te
          yeienhwi eri.
          **(I've sent a message to the
          government asking for more supplies
          and the balance of our money. There
          is nothing else to do.)**

A FRANTIC MOTHER runs to LaSalle.

                    FRANTIC MOTHER
          Chieywannen Armstrong. Ndio yaroye
          ase. Ayiena yenheon.
          **(Chief Armstrong! Please come
          quickly! My child is very sick.)**

                    LASALLE
          Kwioti atiywannen yonkat de
          hachiaaha?
          **(Have the elder women looked at the
          child?)**

                    FRANTIC MOTHER
          Aa-o. Ionnen " Lasalle hese"
          (Yes, and they sent me for you.)

LaSalle follows the woman to her DYING CHILD.

INT. LONG HOUSE - DAY

The child is moaning and racked with fever.

                    DYING CHILD
          Annen-en
          (Mother...)

                    FRANTIC MOTHER
          Xa yendare.
          (I'm here. Right here.)

The woman takes the child's hand and holds it tightly to her chest. LaSalle removes the child's hand and looks at the palm, where a rash covers all but the fingers.

                    LASALLE
Annen haonye ahannonhwa.
(How long has he been like this?)

                  FRANTIC MOTHER
Thora yentaye hoatarihati. Oechaye haonye orahwiye.
(The fever for a few days, but the rash just this morning.)

                    LASALLE
Steniestha tewewentendi i?
(And no one knows what this is?)

                  FRANTIC MOTHER
Stan.
(No.)

The boy coughs and then turns his head to the side revealing a rash covering the side of his face. LaSalle turns to the Tribe Members that are standing in the doorway.

                    LASALLE
Se Otsirayenrat.
(Get White Cloud.)

                WYANDOT WARRIOR
Stan te araskawan. kayahkweyi.
(But she cannot walk or see.)

                    LASALLE
Seatenhawit!.
(Then carry her!)

The Tribe Members run off.

EXT. COUNTRYSIDE - SAME

Little Bird walks with Standing Bear through the woods. She slows and then bends at the waist.

                  LITTLE BIRD
Ahhh...

                  STANDING BEAR
Kwioti achiakwetonde?
(Is it your child?)

                    LITTLE BIRD
          Aa-o.
          (Yes.)

                    STANDING BEAR
          Ehtate tho yandetara askati.
          Chieienhwi echiet i?
          **(There is a clearing beyond those
          pines. Can you make it?)**

Little Bird nods her head. Standing Bear puts his arm under
Little Bird, lifts her up, and guides her to the clearing.

                    LITTLE BIRD
          Onywandouen tioskenhia i?
          (Mother is close?)

                    STANDING BEAR
           Esaatenhaon.
          (We both carry you.)

Little Bird smiles. They walk twenty more yards to a clearing
of soft, tall grass.

Little Bird doubles over in pain, pulling her legs to her
chest. Standing Bear pushes her knees down, places his hand
on her forehead, and begins to chant.

                    STANDING BEAR (cont'd)
              (Chants Wyandot words of
               comfort)

INT. LONGHOUSE - SAME

The Tribe Members appear at the door with WHITE CLOUD, a very
old woman, in their arms. They carry her to LaSalle's side
and place her next to the child.

White Cloud reaches out and grabs at the air for a moment and
then reaching for the blanket wrapped around the child, she
rips it from him. She brings the blanket to her nose.

                    WHITE CLOUD
          Ndio onhwa so
          (You must leave at once.)

                    FRANTIC MOTHER
          Ayiena hawenheon.
          (My child is dying!)

                    WHITE CLOUD
Hechiena ahawenhej. âchie.
(Your child is already dead. You must leave this place.)

                    LASALLE
Onxirihwwandoton. Kwatrihotati d' ondratarion ohkaskwa Wendat yehen.
(We have been told stories of a sickness that spread through the ancient tribes of our people.)

                    WHITE CLOUD

Ondratarion onhwa ohkaskwa, chionyweientia d'haywannen. Aweti de honandiarandi d' haonyweientia âien. Taontaient ashen tendi te kare entaye. Yaro senwharenhaon yenwharaennon.
(And the not so ancient, my young chief. It is the same. All who have come in contact with the boy should be sent away, only to return after twelve suns have passed. Bring the blankets here.)

                    WYANDOT WARRIOR
Yenwharaennon onywannon d'atho.
(They are our only protection from the cold!)

                    WHITE CLOUD
Xkha yenwharaennon onywandet d'yenheon. Senwharenhaon dinde steniestha sateyatannon xa yandataen.
(They are your death wrap. Bring them here and then burn everything inside this place.)

                    DYING CHILD
Annen-en….Tayendet.
(Mother...please hold me.)

                    WHITE CLOUD
Te hechiendet echiehej. Onne, taoten eyaatenk wa chiena?
(Hold him if you must, but you will die in each other's arms. What then becomes of your other child?)

                    FRANTIC MOTHER
          Stan te oatarihati.
          (She has not been touched by the
          fever.)

                    WHITE CLOUD
          Te stan te echiaraskwa eyensok.
          Onhwa ywarihwatendoton a8eti
          esk8enhej d'ondratarion
          sk8andiarandi.
          (If you stay she is surely an
          orphan... for as I sit here I tell
          you all will die that this plague
          touches.)

                    LASALLE
          Chi ayayenk. Aekwaer d'ayenhaon.
          Aweti kha skwandare âskaret
          yarhayon. Tho tsindare ashen tendi
          te kare entaye. Haonye tonteste.
          Taywenwharenhwa Taywatsistenhwa.
          (She has seen this before and we
          must do as she says. All who have
          been in this place must go into the
          woods and wait the twelve suns
          before returning. Bring me the
          blankets and fire.)

The Tribe Member disappears. The Frantic Mother reaches for her child, but LaSalle grabs her arm.

                    FRANTIC MOTHER
          Aiena!
          (My son!)

                    WHITE CLOUD
          Se. Ehechiekwenton hechiena. Xa
          hechiena chehej.
          (Go from this place and you will
          live to bear another son, for this
          child is gone.)

LaSalle stands holding the arm of the Frantic Mother.

                    LASALLE
          Se.
          (You must go.)

                    FRANTIC MOTHER
          Hiena haonhwa âhehej.
          (My child must not die alone.)

> WHITE CLOUD
> Hechiena haonhwa te heheonche.
> Ehendet. eyiwej eaywariskon
> d'hatiyondaskehen.
> **(He will not. I shall hold this boy
> in my arms and together we will
> join our ancestors.)**

LaSalle begins to drag her to the doorway. A Tribe Member returns with a burning torch as others arrive with arm loads of blankets. White Cloud gathers the Dying Child in her arms and holds him against her chest. The boy turns his head and opens his eyes.

> DYING CHILD
> Annen-en
> **(My Mother...)**

> WHITE CLOUD
> Kha indare, ayiena.
> **(I'm here, my child.)**

The blankets are placed in the middle of the longhouse. LaSalle is handed a torch and he places it against the wall of the longhouse and it erupts in flames.

EXT. LONGHOUSE - SAME

LaSalle turns to the Frantic Mother.

> LASALLE
> Onhwa se. Seyenk te skaatat. Ara
> tontase d'aweskwak ashen tendi te
> kare entaye.
> **(Go now and see no one. Return only
> after the twelve suns have passed.)**

The Frantic Mother walks off in a trance. LaSalle looks around at the Wyandot tribe gathered around the longhouse.

> LASALLE (cont'd)
> Yenheon onywariskon. Te asahten
> yahiatonchrenhaon d'ondratarion
> âwet onhwa yarhayon. Aientawa,
> ashen tendi te kare entaye chia
> taontawet. Ayonhwa Âye. Iyerhe
> eywayenk d'aweskwak ashen tendi te
> kare entaye.
> **(A dark death has descended upon
> us. If anyone is seen with the
> signs it carries, they must go
> into the woods alone and stay for
> twelve suns before returning.**
> (MORE)

                    LASALLE (cont'd)
          **I myself must go and hope to see
          you in as many days.)**

                    WYANDOT WARRIOR
          Tsinnen esayorihwatendoton d'
          Chawanonronnon?
          **(Who will represent us with the
          Shawnee?)**

                    LASALLE
          Eyarihwaoka d'ondratarion chia
          eoaka d'ondratarion. Etsungiandika
          tsaten te eonxiandatare.
          **(Word of our plague will spread as
          fast as the sickness. We will not
          be visited soon. Be well.)**

LaSalle walks away and into the woods, the smoke from the
burning longhouse billowing behind him.

EXT. WILDFLOWERS - DAY

Standing Bear and Little Bird, with newborn ELIZA in her
arms, walk in the wildflowers. Little Bird stops and smiles.

                    LITTLE BIRD
          Eyen d'yarontut.
          (I see the tree.)

                    STANDING BEAR
          Achahorenk de tontachie.
          (You found your way back.)

Little Bird turns to her father.

                    LITTLE BIRD
          Stan, onsaokcatenhwa.
          (No, you brought me.)

                    STANDING BEAR
          Chiehenton, ayiena.
          (I followed you, child.)

Little Bird walks on, followed by Standing Bear. They stop at
the edge of the wildflowers and peer out at the cave. Bear
cubs are playing and the mother bear is resting at the cave
entrance.

                    LITTLE BIRD
          Eliza, ayiena. Sakakwa ondechate
          Wendake. Satonnhara d'chionnhase.
                    (MORE)

                    LITTLE BIRD (cont'd)
          **(Eliza my own, look as I did upon
          our homeland and rejoice in your
          new life.)**

                    STANDING BEAR
          Yatoyen ti oskenheati chiewirawan
          yannionyen.
          **(Doesn't it feel wonderful to have
          a bear cub of your own?)**

Little Bird smiles as she lays on the ground, her face basking in the bright sunshine, Eliza wrapped in a blanket across her chest.

                    STANDING BEAR (CONT'D) (cont'd)
          Sandwen onhwa sachiendaen.
          **(Your mother is proud of this
          moment.)**

                    LITTLE BIRD
          Atonronton sonyinnonhwes.
          (She loved us so very much.)

Standing Bear, the wind beginning to blow his silver hair, closes his eyes and slowly nods his head. Opening his eyes, he smiles and reaches out to brush the hair out of Little Bird's eyes.

                    STANDING BEAR
          Haonye chia utarihen, âiaywentawi.
          **(While it is warm, we should
          sleep.)**

EXT. WILDFLOWERS - LATER

The sun has passed behind the fallen tree and the shadows cover the sleeping Little Bird and Eliza. Little Bird begins to awaken, and feeling something behind her ear runs her hand through her hair. Her fingers remove her father's eagle feather.

Little Bird gets to her feet and runs a few steps toward the cave. Standing Bear is stopped at the mouth of the cave.

                    LITTLE BIRD
          Stan, stan, ayisten.
          (No...No, My Father.)

The mother bear is up on her hind legs as she towers over Standing Bear. Little Bird is frozen as the bear attacks her father. Standing Bear makes no sound. Little Bird turns away sobbing, and stumbles into the wildflowers. As she cries she places the eagle feather behind her ear.

                    FLOATING VOICE (V.O.)
          As Little Bird began the long walk
          home she wondered what the gift was
          that her father wanted to leave her
          that day. Was it the memory of her
          mother and the great love they
          shared? Was it the eagle feather
          he cherished so? Was it his death,
          the dignity, the bravery of it all?
          As she slept, her father had said
          his goodbye. She would spend the
          rest of her life saying hers.

INT. FUND RAISER - NIGHT

A marble foyer leads to the banks main hall where a hundred
business suited guest are mingling in conversation. Charles
and Lyda enter the room and immediately there are whispers.

                    LYDA
          At least they know we're here.

LIBBY AND MARY MCKAY, twin spinster sisters, walk up to
Charles and Lyda.

                    MARY MCKAY
          Senator how are you?

                    CHARLES CURTIS
          I'm wonderful, Mary, and how have
          you and Libby been getting along?

                    MARY MCKAY
          Other than her trying to steal my
          love interests, we're getting along
          quite nicely.

                    LYDA
          Hello I'm Lyda...

Lyda extends her hand.

                    CHARLES CURTIS
                (interrupting)
          Oh, I'm sorry. Mary and Libby
          McKay, this is Lyda Conley.

                    LIBBY MCKAY
          Oh we know. You and your sisters
          are quite the scandal around the
          bridge table. How are you dear?

LYDA
Fine I thought...

MARY MCKAY
These stick in the muds could use a good ole' kick in the backside. From what I've read, you're just the woman to give it to them.

CHARLES CURTIS
From what I've seen I would agree.

LIBBY MCKAY
And you young man, Another term for you I hope.

CHARLES CURTIS
That's why we're here.

MARY MCKAY
I thought we were here to catch up on the gossip.

Libby pulls both Charles and Lyda close.

LIBBY MCKAY
Randolph has had his staff out getting signatures for a run at the seat as well. You'll win, but he is a power broker. Could make your life a little easier should he decide not to run.

CHARLES CURTIS
Thank you.

MARY MCKAY
The thanks are to you for bringing this breath of fresh air into this very stuffy party. Oh my! I see a very handsome stranger at the door. You stay and keep Charles and Lyda company, Lib and I'll be right back.

Mary walks off.

LIBBY MCKAY
That's no stranger, that's the college president!

Libby steps quickly to join her sister.

                    LYDA
          They're quite the pair.

                    CHARLES CURTIS
          They're the sisters of Cyrus McKay,
          the steamboat company owner. I pity
          the person that breaks up that
          relationship.

                    LYDA
          Senator, I believe that is Randolph
          Johnson waving at you.

                    CHARLES CURTIS
          You must call me Charles.

                    LYDA
          No... I must call you Senator.

Charles nods then looks up and sees Randolph Johnson standing
beside his aristocratic wife ELIZABETH JOHNSON.

                    CHARLES CURTIS
          Into the mouth of the lion we go.

Charles takes Lyda's arm and walks across the ballroom floor.
People step out of the way and look as they walk. Behind
them, the guests close the gap and an audible murmur escapes
into the room. As they approach the Johnson's, the people
begin to drift away from the two couples.

                    RANDOLPH JOHNSON
          You're not going to keep this
          pretty lady all to yourself are
          you?

                    CHARLES CURTIS
          Certainly not from you, Randolph.
          Lyda Conley, this is Randolph and
          Elizabeth Johnson. They own most of
          the land around Kansas City.

                    LYDA
          That is wonderful I'm sure. But it
          causes me pause.

                    ELIZABETH JOHNSON
          Why is that dear?

                    LYDA
          If your family owns most of the
          land around Kansas City, why are
          you so interested in the two acres
          my ancestors rest in?

67.

> RANDOLPH JOHNSON
> That's quite the opening statement. You may want to rephrase it.

> CHARLES CURTIS
> I thought the question was well defined.

Lyda locks eyes with Johnson.

> LYDA
> Well?

> ELIZABETH JOHNSON
> It's alright. It's her Indian spirit talking.

> LYDA
> You don't know my spirit, ma'am. But yours is very clear to see.

Lyda walks off.

> ELIZABETH JOHNSON
> Did you really expect anything civilized to find its way out of her mouth?

> CHARLES CURTIS
> With all due respect, Elizabeth.

> ELIZABETH JOHNSON
> Is that the excuse for your choice of companions? Everyone knows you're part Indian.

Charles just turns and walks away.

> ELIZABETH JOHNSON (CONT'D) (cont'd)
> And where is Mrs. Curtis? Home with the children while...

Charles slows his stride. Randolph steps in front of his wife and stops her in mid sentence.

Charles resumes toward Lyda once Elizabeth is silenced. He reaches Lyda's side as she looks out at the faint light coming from inside Fort Conley.

> CHARLES CURTIS
> Now that was a first impression.

Charles follows Lyda's eyes and looks out toward Fort Conley.

                    CHARLES CURTIS (cont'd)
          That shack has become a symbol.

                    LYDA
          You know there is no heat or water.
          We take turns so none of us suffers
          more than the other. Sometimes we
          all stay just to be sure we make it
          one more night.

Lyda opens the glass door and a gust of wind whips through
the hall. All eyes turn to Lyda and Charles. Someone steps up
and closes the door.

                    MICHAEL BYRON
          Senator!

MICHAEL BYRON, one of the government's attorneys in Lyda's
case removes his hand from the door handle.

                    CHARLES CURTIS
          Michael... what is it.

                    MICHAEL BYRON
          Actually, I would like to speak to
          your guest.

Charles steps back in surprise at Michael's comment.

                    MICHAEL BYRON (cont'd)
          One of my cases involved Miss
          Conley.

                    LYDA
          You refer to the case in the past
          tense, Mr. Byron. Certainly...

                    MICHAEL BYRON
              (interrupting)
          You haven't been notified?

                    LYDA
          Of what?

                    MICHAEL BYRON
          We got the notice in our offices
          this afternoon. The judge denied
          your appeal. I'm afraid it's over.

                    LYDA
          That can't be. I just filed the
          appeal this morning.

Lyda looks at Charles and Charles at Michael.

MICHAEL BYRON
Why are you looking at me like that? This isn't anything personal. It's just a case. Obviously it was the judge's decision, not mine.

Charles stiffens. When the onslaught from Lyda never comes, he turns to her. Lyda stands, tears welling in her eyes.

MICHAEL BYRON (cont'd)
I'm sorry, Charles. Sorry Miss Conley.

Michael leaves and then Lyda, wiping her eyes opens the door and steps out into the cold.

EXT. FUND RAISER - NIGHT

CHARLES CURTIS
Your coat.

Lyda keeps walking.

CHARLES CURTIS (cont'd)
Lyda, wait. Please.

Charles quickens his pace and catches her.

LYDA
They won. They always win. Don't you realize we're the Wyandot? The peaceful warriors.

Lyda keeps walking toward Fort Conley.

INT. FORT CONLEY - LATER

Lena rolled inside a blanket is asleep in the corner of Fort Conley. Ida sits cross legged, her eyes piercing the door. Lyda opens the door and taking off her shoes steps inside.

IDA
So?

Lyda looks surprised at Ida's greeting.

LYDA
I was out.

IDA
Maybe you should be out a little less and working a little more.

LYDA
It's all I've done for a year! Are you insane?

IDA
No but everyone thinks I am.

LYDA
It's not your fault.

IDA
They said I was the cause of them losing the government contract.

LYDA
You? Don't you mean Lena and me?

Lena gets up and leans forward.

LYDA (cont'd)
And you want us to stop so you can get your job back?

IDA
No. I was the only one that got paid every week. Now what? We need money for food... we need money to live.

LENA
No we don't.

IDA
That's because Lyda and I have always helped you.

LENA
And when you were sick or sad who was by your side? And not just me. Are you forgetting we are not alone here.

IDA
Oh, is the dead Summunduwatt going to rise up and cook you a hot meal?

LYDA
Ida stop!

IDA
Stop it yourself! Look at us? It's ten degrees and we might as well be outside.
(MORE)

                    IDA (cont'd)
We were happy before all of this. I
had a job, slept in a bed, we had a
real life!

                    LENA
A life of what? Sending messages on
a wire? What message can you send
by standing guard for those that
can't.

                    IDA
You are both so stubborn! I am
telling you we are in trouble.

There is a silent moment.

                    LYDA
We lost the case today.

                    LENA
You what?

                    LYDA
Me? I said WE lost the case.

                    IDA
You're the lawyer, not me or her! I
haven't been living in this hat box
for nothing! You need to do
something, now.

                    LYDA
I've filed an appeal. I had it
ready in case we lost.

                    LENA
That was your first mistake. You
never should have considered losing
Lyda. Never consider losing.

                    LYDA
I did good work on those papers!

                    LENA
We will never learn... They just
keep making papers and we keep
signing papers and pointing at the
signatures on those papers and then
they change the papers and make a
new paper that we sign again. It is
their greatest weapon against us
and it always has been.

LYDA
We have to find a way to stop this.

LENA
You do as you want... but don't forget that they created the legal system and you more than anyone should understand that. They created it so they could control it. Me... I'm going to stay right here where I control what happens.

IDA
Lena you need to stop looking at this like some childs' game. They want this land. Do you really think that you and Lyda Conley stand a chance if the great tribes and their chiefs, Sitting Bull, Crazy Horse and Geronimo did not.

LENA
I said it before... we are not alone and in the flesh we may suffer but in the spirit we will win.

IDA
Suffer yes... win no.

LENA
You don't see what I see when I walk here. There is not only the Wayandots standing with us... but also the Apache, Cherokee and Sioux.

IDA
Then let them sleep here and fight this ridiculous fight. I'm going home.

Ida walks out the door.

LENA
And why didn't you say something?

LYDA
She knew she was listening to us all.

EXT. WYANDOT KANSAS VILLAGE - DAY

With Eliza across her chest Little Bird walks into the village that seems deserted. She notices the burned ashes of the Longhouse and stops.

                    LITTLE BIRD
LaSalle?

Slowly, people begin to appear. A YOUNG WYANDOT GIRL approaches Little Bird.

                    YOUNG WYANDOT GIRL
Haywannen ehrehti yarhayon.
(The Chief has gone into the woods.)

                    LITTLE BIRD
Taot endi?
(What happened?)

                    YOUNG WYANDOT GIRL
Ondratarion ayonywandathara. Wich iwahsen hendenhej. Ayendwen ayenhaon tiawenk. Ayenhaon Lasalle hateihtha. Ayenhaon onnianni sonywahente. Ayenhaon Serihwandoton d' ahaatenha.
(A plague has come upon us. Fifty have died. My mother has sent me to thank you for LaSalle's brave guidance and tell you of his fate.)

                    LITTLE BIRD
Ahaatenha.
(His fate?)

                    YOUNG WYANDOT GIRL
Hawyannen ahahente hoyen ayitakhen. Yatoyen hondrori ondratarion. Aret yarhayon enta8an ashen tendi te kare entaye. Ara ayendwen dinde skat hoskenrayehte tontahnde.
(The Chief was the first to see my brother and certainly he was covered in the sickness. He, like the others, went into the woods for twelve suns. Only my mother and a single warrior have returned.)

                    LITTLE BIRD
Annen ehawehti?.
(Where did he go?)

                    YOUNG WYANDOT GIRL
          Ahtiawenre yaienton.
          (No one was allowed to follow.)

Little Bird, cradling Eliza, drops to her knees. The Young Wyandot Girl helps her back on her feet.

                    YOUNG WYANDOT GIRL (CONT'D) (cont'd)
          Chiorendich. Ndio sendiahay.
          **(You must be hungry, come and eat
          with us.)**

Little Bird pulls away and hands Eliza to a waiting elder.

                    LITTLE BIRD
          Sennon ayiena.
          (Care for my child.)

Little Bird begins to run, following the same path as LaSalle. She runs up a hillside to the plateau.

EXT. WYANDOT KANSAS VILLAGE - HILL - DAY

Little Bird takes the last few steps up a steep incline and then stops as she reaches the top. LaSalle is sitting on the rock overlooking the Wyandot village. Little Bird runs to him.

                    LITTLE BIRD
          Lasalle, kha endare. Lasalle
          (LaSalle! I'm here! LaSalle.)

LaSalle raises his hand.

                    LASALLE
          Ennon ese.
          (Come no closer.)

Little Bird stops a few feet from him. LaSalle looks weak, his eyes sunken, his skin pale and his lips parched. She is first in shock and then understanding she needs to be strong smiles.

                    LITTLE BIRD
          Yanderati yonnonhwes. Stan te
          chiennonhwandi.
          (Oh, my great love you are well.)

LaSalle turns his head slightly but his eyes are blank.

                    LASALLE
          Yonehiera.
          (I have been waiting for you.)

                    LITTLE BIRD
          Ayonehwandik, yonnonhwes. I,erhe
          eyonatenhwa onyiondaon sti echiyenk
          kwaiena.
          **(I've missed you my love. I've come
          to take you home to be with our
          daughter.)**

                    LASALLE
          Thora enta8an stan te yiatoristi
          sti yonehiera.
          **(For days I've not moved waiting
          for you to come.)**

Little Bird opens the blanket around her and LaSalle sees
that her pregnancy is over.

                    LITTLE BIRD
          Ndio ekwet. Saatawan askennonia
          oskenrayehte eawehti
          **(Let us go. Your peaceful warrior
          has come.)**

                    LASALLE
          Onnianni serihwaiensten. Yaro
          eyandare eyontahkwi.
          **(Teach her well, for this is where
          I'll stay.)**

                    LITTLE BIRD
          Stan.
          (No!)

Little Bird begins to weep uncontrollably. LaSalle with his
remaining strength extends his arms and turns his palms
toward Little Bird.

                    LASALLE
          Yaro ase yandaye.
          (Join me at the river.)

LaSalle's arms fall to his side and his head falls to the
side as his eyes close and he dies.

                                        FADE TO BLACK.

EXT. HURON CEMETARY - NIGHT

In the stark moonlight the rock where LaSalle died can
clearly be seen, now overgrown with weeds. The silence is
broken by laughter and the closing of a door. Now in the
distance city streets with gas lamps and tall buildings
surround LaSalle's last resting place.

MONTAGE - SEASONS PASS

INT. PARLOR - DAY

Ida irons in a beautiful parlor as an aristocratic woman drops more clothes at her feet.

INT. FORT CONLEY - NIGHT

Lena reads a fortune under candle light.

INT. LIBRARY - DAY

Lyda writes in the library.

INT. FORT CONLEY - DAY

Lena counts the money in the war chest.

EXT. WYANDOT CEMETARY - DAY

The grass, now brown and parched, lays flat in the windless summer heat. A group of construction workers are standing around looking at the fence that surrounds Fort Conley. The PAVING CONTRACTOR pushes one of the workers to the side and grabs a fence post.

                    PAVING CONTRACTOR
          What are you waiting for?

The Contractor begins pulling on the fence post and it lifts out easily. He pulls out another and another. A side of the fence collapses. He reaches for another corner post. Other workers jump in and quickly begin taking the fence down and carting it off. A small line of five posts and wire remain

Lena walks past the men and enters the shack.

The Paving Contractor steps past his men and rips another post out of the ground.

                    PAVING CONTRACTOR (cont'd)
          Let me have the pleasure.

                    PAVING ASSISTANT CONTRACTOR
          Hey boss.

                    PAVING CONTRACTOR
          What?

                    PAVING ASSISTANT CONTRACTOR
          You better not.

                    PAVING CONTRACTOR
          What?

The Paving Contractor spins to face his assistant and instead is looking down the barrel of Lena's shotgun. Lena has one eye closed and the other directly over the gun.

                    PAVING CONTRACTOR (cont'd)
          You don't scare me with that old
          rusted piece of pipe.

The contractor turns and places his hand on the post. His hand rests on the top without moving. Lena fires the shotgun a few feet above his head. He never says anything but the post is moving with the rhythm of his shaking hand.

                    LENA
          You touch one more post and they'll
          be using them to make a cross for
          your grave.

The Paving Contractor slowly lifts his hand from the post. Sweating in the hot morning air, the contractor walks off, followed by his men.

EXT. FORT CONLEY - LATER

Lena walks down the hill and into the streets of Kansas City. The Paving Contractor watching from a distance steps from behind a large truck. He walks up the hillside and he and his men begin to dismantle the final fence posts.

Lyda steps to the doorway and raises the shotgun. The Assistant hits his boss on the arm and points toward the fort. The Paving Contractor looks up surprised.

                    PAVING CONTRACTOR
          How many of you are there?

                    LYDA
          Thousands.

The Paving Contractor shakes his head and again makes his way out of the cemetary.

EXT. FORT CONLEY - LATER

Lyda goes inside and retrieving the War Chest, she returns outside. Lyda removes several bills and hands them to Lena.

                    LYDA
          This is the last of it, but it
          should pay for two rolls of wire
          and twenty-four posts.

                    LENA
          We need half this much.

                    LYDA
          This won't be the last time we
          build it.

INT. RESTAURANT - AFTERNOON

Senator Charles Curtis sits alone reading a newspaper and sipping an ice tea.

A Disturbed Randolph Johnson strides into the restaurant and slides into a chair across Curtis. Curtis lowers his paper.

                    RANDOLPH JOHNSON
          Tell me something Charles, what is
          it that these women want? Money?
          Whatever I end up paying the
          government I'll match it and pay
          the same to them. They want to keep
          it or share it with the rest of
          the...whatever they're called.

                    CHARLES CURTIS
          Wyandot. They are the Wyandot,
          Randolph.

                    RANDOLPH JOHNSON
          First they run off Whitaker and now
          I can't even get a damn sidewalk
          built to my office. You know they
          rebuilt that fence eleven times!
          It's costing me a fortune to get
          nothing done!

                    CHARLES CURTIS
          What you want, they can't give you.

Startled, Randolph leans over the table.

                    RANDOLPH JOHNSON
          Yes they can. I want that land.

                    CHARLES CURTIS
          It's not theirs to give. It belongs
          to the people that are buried
          there.

RANDOLPH JOHNSON
Dead people don't own anything.

CHARLES CURTIS
You're finding out the hard way that they do.

RANDOLPH JOHNSON
I've had about enough of this. From them and from you. I dropped my candidacy so you would show me some appreciation. I can see you have no intention of helping me with this.

CHARLES CURTIS
You haven't asked me to help you with anything. You storm uninvited during my peaceful lunch and start ranting about the Conley sisters. You want my help? I'm telling you that you're wasting your time.

RANDOLPH JOHNSON
What?

CHARLES CURTIS
That wasn't clear?

RANDOLPH JOHNSON
It's clear that you have fallen under some spell this young woman cast on you. There are rumors...

CHARLES CURTIS
You just don't understand.

RANDOLPH JOHNSON
I understand perfectly.

CHARLES CURTIS
No, Randolph you don't understand. This isn't about being in love with Lyda Conley, or money, or power.

Randolph stands and looks at Curtis.

RANDOLPH JOHNSON
I didn't get to own half this state by playing fair. They're about to find out whose table they're at.

Randolph stands and slowly walks off.

                    CHARLES CURTIS
          Well you better set another plate
          because I'm joining them at your
          table.

EXT. LIBRARY - LATER

Charles sits on a bench across from the library. Lyda exits
and Charles approaches her.

                    CHARLES CURTIS
          Lyda.

Lyda looks, smiles and walks to Curtis.

                    CHARLES CURTIS (cont'd)
          I'm leaving for Washington, do you
          have a moment.

                    LYDA
          Yes.

                    CHARLES CURTIS
          I wanted to say goodbye and tell
          you that I will do whatever I can
          for you and your efforts.

                    LYDA
          Thank you. You know that Randolph
          has sent messengers with offers?

                    CHARLES CURTIS
          Yes. He just made it clear to me
          that he has made his last offer.

                    LYDA
          I can't be distracted by him. I am
          focused on the court.

                    CHARLES CURTIS
          With my reelection campaign I will
          not be back this way for awhile.

Charles and Lyda stare for a moment, each knowing that in
another place and time this relationship would have been
different. That they would have fallen into each others arms.
But that was not to be. Charles and Lyda had been important
to each other in this place and time and that was more than
either could have hoped.

Charles steps forward and hands a card to Lyda he then opens
his arms to give Lyda a hug.

                    CHARLES CURTIS (cont'd)
          It's just a note.

Lyda lets his arms enfold her and she closes her eyes to
imagine... Charles is doing the same. They each move away at
the same moment and without another word Charles is gone.

EXT. KANSAS CITY STREET - AFTERNOON

Lyda stands in the shadow of a tree and opens Charles note.

                    CHARLES CURTIS (V.O.)
          Dearest Lyda, with this note, I
          keep a silent promise to Sarah. As
          I turned from her grave that first
          day, she asked me to tell you how
          proud she is of her baby sisters.
          She is with you always, and I will
          be as well, Charles.

Lyda tucks the letter into a dress pocket and then leans on
the broken fence and looks up toward the window of Charles
Curtis' office. He is not there.

INT. RANDOLPH JOHNSON'S OFFICE - DAY

Whitaker and Johnson are looking at landscape drawings as
MICHAEL FOSTER enters and sits.

                    RANDOLPH JOHNSON
          You've spoken to Landon?

                    MICHAEL FOSTER
          Last week, Randolph.

                    RANDOLPH JOHNSON
          And?

                    MICHAEL FOSTER
          No one can help her. I'm the only
          attorney in the state that can.
          Now, if we need to keep meeting on
          this Conley mess I'm going to start
          billing you.

                    RANDOLPH JOHNSON
          Do as you wish. I'll write the
          check out of your partnership
          proceeds. Look at Whitaker's plans
          so we can approve the design. He
          thinks we can get two, maybe three
          buildings on the site.

                    MICHAEL FOSTER
          Not four?

                    RANDOLPH JOHNSON
          I knew there was a reason I liked
          you.

Whitaker erases a small park and draws a square building.

INT. FORT CONLEY - MORNING

Lyda and Lena are asleep as rain pelts Fort Conley. In the distance a clock tower strikes seven times. Lyda jumps up from the floor, grabs a coat and an umbrella.

                    LENA
          Where are you going?

                    LYDA
          I have an appointment at eight!

                    LENA
          The great women that came before us
          will be watching.

EXT. FORT CONLEY - MORNING

She starts out, but remembers her papers and tucks them under her coat. The wind immediately turns her umbrella inside out. She struggles and forces it back in shape.

Lyda makes her way slowly down the hillside, but loses her footing and begins to slide. She drops the umbrella to cushion her fall, but lands hard on her side. She slides down the side of the muddy hill stopping in a puddle. Her papers are dry, but she is soaked and covered in mud.

EXT. LANDON LAW BUILDING - MOMENTS LATER

Lyda stands, looking up at the twenty stairs leading to the double brass doors of the Landon Law Building. With a deep breath, she begins walking up the stairs toward the door.

INT. LANDON LAW BUILDING - MOMENTS LATER

Lyda stands in the foyer of the Landon Law building looking at a legal directory. Lawyers and their clients avoid the lone figure as Lyda looks at the dirty water dripping around her feet. Slowly, she begins to walk down the hallway and then walks up a circular set of marble stairs.

At the top of the stairs is a granite reception area. As Lyda steps toward LANDON'S SECRETARY, the woman looks up, smiles, and points toward an open ornate oak doorway.

Lyda enters. GEORGE LANDON, sixties, thick silver hair and a moustache, rises, pulls a chair out for Lyda. He extends his hand.

      GEORGE LANDON
  Miss Conley, welcome.

Lyda looks down at her dirty hand and wipes it on her dress before shaking his hand.

      GEORGE LANDON (cont'd)
  I've been following your petition
  since it's first day in court. I
  told Senator Curtis of my interest
  in helping. I assumed by your
  letter that he passed that along?

      LYDA
  Yes he did.

      GEORGE LANDON
  I know this place seems formal, but
  please relax. We represent clients
  that expect us to maintain a
  certain... image.

      LYDA
  Even with my battle against Mother
  Nature clearly lost, I'm quite
  comfortable Mr. Landon. I want to
  thank you for this audience.

      GEORGE LANDON
  Please call me George. Before I
  convinced everyone of my legal
  acumen I was a clerk in a
  Washington law firm.

      LYDA
  I know that, Mr...I'm sorry,
  George. That's why I sent my papers
  in advance.

      GEORGE LANDON
  As Cicero tells us, "equal and
  exact justice to all men under the
  law."

      LYDA
  That's my problem.

GEORGE LANDON
Lets discuss, as you say, your papers. You have a creative legal mind. You blend both traditional principles of contract and constitutional law, and apply them to the history of your people. Simply brilliant.

LYDA
Thank you.

GEORGE LANDON
However, I'm afraid that all your brilliant verbiage will fall upon very deaf ears.

LYDA
Why?

GEORGE LANDON
In the United States, Congress makes laws, not God. And in 1871, the U.S. Congress stated that Indian tribes were not sovereign nations and were incapable of making treaties with the federal government. And as you may or may not know, there is a precedent on this question.

LYDA
Lone Wolf vs. Hitchcock, among others.

GEORGE LANDON
In that case, the court held that the U.S. Government can repeal a treaty through federal legislation.

LYDA
But if I have no rights to the land granted by the treaty, then I have no argument.

GEORGE LANDON
Now you know the difficulty you face.

LYDA
I have to get to the Supreme Court. It's the only hope we have. I know I can get them to see how wrong those decisions were.
(MORE)

                    LYDA (cont'd)
Perhaps they'll overturn the
precedents if I argue moral
imperatives.

                    GEORGE LANDON
Legislation is not always moral,
Miss Conley.

                    LYDA
Nor justice equal and exact. I need
you to vouch for my character with
the Supreme Court.

                    GEORGE LANDON
That I can't. With all my legal
history it seems I am not approved
by the court in Washington.
However, there is a man who can.
His name is Michael Foster. He
practices law in Washington. I
believe he is approved by the High
Court and has set up a temporary
office in Kansas City. He's over on
State Street.

                    LYDA
You've been very kind, George.

                    GEORGE LANDON
Sorry I couldn't have been of more
assistance, however I believe you
know what you need to do.

                    LYDA
Thank you.

Lyda gets up, shakes George's hand and walks out.

INT. MICHAEL FOSTER'S OFFICES - DAY - ONE WEEK LATER

Lyda sits in a waiting area reading. MICHAEL FOSTER'S
SECRETARY walks up.

                    MICHAEL FOSTER'S SECRETARY
Miss Conley.

                    LYDA
Yes.

                    MICHAEL FOSTER'S SECRETARY
I'm sorry, but Mister Foster can't
keep his appointment with you
today.

LYDA
Is there an emergency? I'd be happy to return later today.

MICHAEL FOSTER'S SECRETARY
Not an emergency, just a scheduling conflict.

LYDA
I did make the appointment a week ago.

The Secretary sits down next to Lyda.

MICHAEL FOSTER'S SECRETARY
(whispering)
I read in the paper about you and your sisters. I want you to know my women's club supports you.

Lyda nods.

MICHAEL FOSTER'S SECRETARY (cont'd)
So this is hard for me. Mister Foster isn't going to meet with you.

LYDA
He has to!

MICHAEL FOSTER'S SECRETARY
Shhhh... Please. I'll be fired. I was told to reschedule you for two weeks.

LYDA
That's fine. I can wait.

MICHAEL FOSTER'S SECRETARY
He's leaving for Washington this Saturday. He will never see you. I'm sorry.

Lyda gets up and placing the newspaper back in her case, begins to walk off.

FLOATING VOICE (V.O.)
The warrior within you must rise and be felt.

Lyda turns and storms toward an office door. Lyda never flinches as she throws the door open. Michael Foster sits at his desk and looks up startled.

MICHAEL FOSTER
How the hell!

RANDOLPH JOHNSON (O.S.)
You say something, Michael?

Lyda walks to Michael Foster's desk. He recoils.

LYDA
With or without you I will be heard.

Randolph Johnson steps to the conference room door.

MICHAEL FOSTER
I'm sorry, Randolph. Miss Conley, please excuse yourself and get out of my office.

Lyda spins to face Johnson.

LYDA
Nothing to say about my spirit today, Mister Johnson?

RANDOLPH JOHNSON
Your spirit and your silly fort are no longer a concern of mine.

Lyda turns back to Foster.

LYDA
George Landon spoke so kindly of you. Why won't you help me?

MICHAEL FOSTER
I have no interest in my name being used to waste the Supreme Court's time. I read the outline for your argument and it's amateurish at best. Moral imperatives! You must think this is a fairy-tale you're in.

Lyda lowers her voice and stands tall.

LYDA
I know this isn't a fairy-tale. It is a nightmare. One I promise will not end... for either of you.

Lyda walks out of the office down a hall and into the street.

EXT. MICHAEL FOSTER'S OFFICES - DAY

As Lyda walks toward Fort Conley she hears screams and people running. She looks up to see smoke coming from the cemetery. Lyda begins to run.

EXT. FORT CONLEY - DAY

As she turns the corner there are twenty Kansas City policemen surrounding a bonfire in the street. Lena keeps trying to break through their ranks, but is pushed back. Lyda arrives.

                LYDA
  Lena!

Lena turns.

                LENA
  They tricked me!

                LYDA
  Who did?

                LENA
  Someone called me outside by name
  and said that you were hurt. That
  you had fallen on the courthouse
  stairs. I went to help you. Lyda,
  they ripped it apart and threw it
  into the street! They're burning
  the fort!

Lyda goes to the police.

                LYDA
  By what right are you doing this?

The POLICE CAPTAIN hands Lyda a file.

              POLICE CAPTAIN
  We were given these papers proving
  that you have no right to stop the
  sale of this property and by
  trespassing you are doing so.

                LYDA
  You have no right to do this. I
  have sixty days to file with the
  courts before you can get near this
  property.

The Police Captain smiles and begins to walk away. Fort Conley, the smoke dying away, lays in ashes.

                  POLICE CAPTAIN
     Let's go men.

                  LENA (O.S.)
     You there!

Everyone turns to see Lena now standing above them on the rock jutting out from the hill. She has fire in her eyes and a crystal ball held high in her hand.

                  LENA (cont'd)
     The government you represent has
     broken every treaty they've made
     with the Indians. We have been
     driven from place to place, until
     even our dead are not allowed to
     rest in peace!

Ida appears on Lena's left followed by Lyda on her right. The three sisters standing together the suns fading red light passing between them.

                  LENA (cont'd)
     Cursed be the villains that molest
     their graves!

Lena throws the crystal ball toward the police. It shatters into a thousand pieces at their feet. They look up once more through the smoke of the burning fort.

                  LENA (cont'd)
     All you have done today is send
     smoke signals to the spirits of our
     ancestors!

                  LYDA
     As you see them torment our
     ancestors are you not asking are my
     mother and father next? What is the
     will of this government... If they
     choose they come to your resting
     place and scream... Rip their
     spirits from the earth! Thrown them
     in a truck and carte them to a
     place they never set foot on! Dear
     God... My sixteen year old sister
     is in this ground.

Lyda, eyes burning with passion walks down the hill toward the waiting crowd. Lena and Ida follow. Lyda walks up to one of the men and grabs his shovel. She turns to a citizen.

                    LYDA (cont'd)
          You! Take me to where your
          grandmother rests! Let's dig up her
          bones!

Lyda whips around to face another citizen while raising the shovel in both hands.

                    LYDA (cont'd)
          And you! I want to turn over the
          earth where your father rests! Take
          me to them!

Lyda drops to her knees resting her shoulder against the shovel. She begins to cry.

                    LYDA (cont'd)
               (her voice lowering)
          Let's dig up all your dead
          ancestors!

The people slowly begin to back away as do the officials. Ida and Lena place their hands on Lyda.

EXT. HURON CEMETARY - NIGHT

Lena and Lyda are sitting on a low stone wall a hundred feet from where the fort once stood.

                    LENA
          We have no more money.

                    LYDA
          Why do you think mother told us of
          Little Bird and Lasalle. Why she
          talked about their love for the
          land and each other. The sacrifice
          they made for the tribe. A thousand
          miles of travel and a hundred
          thousand tears cast along the way.
          What have we suffered that they did
          not ten fold. We cannot end this...
          we have to find a way.

                    LENA
          Smoke signals.

                    LYDA
          What?

Lena points to the walkway through the cemetary. Lyda looks over to see Ida walking in front of fifty men, women and children with wood boards, tools and lit torches.

EXT. HURON CEMETARY - DAY

James Whitaker, Durant and the Police Captain arrive again with twenty armed policemen.

                  H.B. DURANT
    Whitaker this is the last chance to
    resolve this. Tomorrow your
    commission ends with the
    government. Looks to me as if
    they've won this battle.

                  JAMES WHITAKER
    Twenty four hours is a long time
    and I'm going to make sure they
    don't come back.

Walking side by side the three men make their way toward Fort Conley. The line of police follow a few steps behind. They stop outside the gate.

                  POLICE CAPTAIN
    We know you can see us. You must
    leave this property at once.

Slowly the door opens and Lena walks out alone.

                  LENA
    Has my sister been injured again
    Captain?

                  POLICE CAPTAIN
    Miss Conley we don't want any
    trouble with you. They have the
    right to sell this land and you're
    going to have to leave now.

Whitaker leans over and whispers into Durant's ear.

                  JAMES WHITAKER
      (softly)
    What is that in the window?

Durant looks around the Police Captain and squints his eyes.

                  H.B. DURANT
    I think it's a chain.

                  LENA
    I'm not going anywhere.

The Police Captain motions for his men to move forward. As they get closer Lena begins to back up. They take a step closer and she takes a step back.

The police now see clearly a chain that is run through the front door's window and then back into the Fort.

                  POLICE CAPTAIN
        That's enough. Go get them out.

Lena throws herself through the door and slams it but the chain stops it from closing. Ten police try and pry the door open but it is difficult, finally they get it open and few of the men make it inside. POLICEMAN #1 sticks his head outside the door.

                  POLICEMAN #1
        She's alone!

                  JAMES WHITAKER
        Then get her out! What's going on
        in there.

Whitaker runs through the fence. And stops as four police, one on each arm and leg bring Lena out.

                  JAMES WHITAKER (cont'd)
        Oh God...

Lena has the thick chain wrapped around her waist a few times and a huge padlock holding it in place. She is chained to the door. Durant shakes his head and just walks off.

                  JAMES WHITAKER (cont'd)
        What is going on?

                  POLICEMAN #1
        Can't you see... she's chained to
        the door.

                  JAMES WHITAKER
        Unlock it you idiot!

                  POLICEMAN #1
        I can't... she swallowed the key.

Whitaker looks over at Lena, his face flushed and then he buries his face in his hands and talks into the ground.

                  JAMES WHITAKER
        Remove the door and take her and
        the door to jail.

EXT. FORT CONLEY - CONTINUOUS

Whitaker watches from a distance as six policemen hoist the door onto their shoulders with Lena sitting upright her hair catching a breeze as if she were on a magic carpet.

The Police Captain and the remaining men stand waiting for Whitaker to move on. Instead he begins ripping the fence posts out of the ground and throwing them in all directions.

He takes a fence post and throws it at the shack.

          JAMES WHITAKER
Take their personal belongings and put them off to the side. Then put these fence posts inside and burn it to the ground!

INT. KANSAS CITY JAIL - AFTERNOON

The door that Lena is chained to leans against the jail house wall. Lena is resting on a hard bench. A policeman opens the cell door and Lyda enters.

          LYDA
That's an interesting piece of jewelry.

          LENA
You should have seen Whitaker's face.

          LYDA
They burned the Fort again.

          LENA
You could be a little nicer... I'm the one in jail.

          LYDA
I just don't know what to do. They will be back again tomorrow and what then? We have to find a way to stop them.

          LENA
We are. It was over two years ago that we stayed our first night and to this day nothing has happened.

Lyda looks around.

                    LYDA
          How are we suppose to get you out
          of this they said you swallowed the
          key.

                    LENA
          Did you pay the fine?

                    LYDA
          Of course I did.

Lena reaches into her dress pocket and removes a key. Lyda
laughs.

                    LENA
          No wonder we keep them away...
          they're fools.

Lena unlocks the padlock and lets the chain fall to the
floor. Together they walk out.

                    POLICEMAN # 2
          Wait! Hold on! What about the door.

Lena goes back and gets the chain and lock.

                    LENA
          You can have the door... it's a
          souvenir for James Whitaker.

INT. CONLEY KANSAS CITY HOME - NIGHT

Lena and Ida are sitting in the kitchen. Lyda her hair still
wet from her shower sits at the table with them.

                    IDA
          How much money do we need to file
          the Supreme Court Papers?

                    LYDA
          It's not just the filing fee. You
          have no idea how much it costs just
          to produce the copies and send the
          documents. It's hundreds of
          dollars.

                    IDA
          I'm working six days a week.

                    LENA
          You know how much I have.

                    LYDA
          Lucy Armstrongs daughter Ellen has
          been inviting me to the suffrage
          meetings at her home. I think maybe
          I need to attend.

                    IDA
          It's come to passing the hat.

                    LYDA
          As long as the moon shall rise...As
          long as the river shall flow... as
          long as the sun shall shine and as
          long as the grass shall grow we
          must do whatever we can. This is
          our trusted duty.

The three sisters look knowingly at each other. Lena reaches
behind her chair and removes a rolled blanket.

                    LENA
          I'll go.

                    IDA & LENA
          We'll all go.

EXT. HURON CEMETARY - NIGHT

The streets are empty as the three sisters walk past the bank
building and up the hill toward the cemetery. In the
brilliant moon lit night the clear outline of the rebuilt
fort can be seen. The sisters begin to run, tears of joy flow
as they reach the erected fence. Opening the gate they see a
basket full of bread and jam as well as a note resting
against the door to Fort Conley.

Lyda turns so the paper faces the moon as the three read.

                    FLOATING VOICE (V.O.)
          A hundred generations have
          delivered you to us. We bless you
          with the tears of those that came
          before and we of today stand with
          you... always.

EXT. 1909 ELLEN ARMSTRONGS' GARDEN - DAY

Twenty women sit in garden chairs as Lyda and ELLEN ARMSTRONG
sits beside her. The woman talk among themselves as Lyda
nervously looks around and keeps bringing the water glass to
her lips to stave off her dry mouth.

                    GUEST #1
               (whispering)
          That's the Conley girl.

                    GUEST #2
               (whispering)
          She says she's a Wayandot... did
          you know her father was white?

                    GUEST #1
          I did hear that.

                    ELLEN ARMSTRONG
          Quite please.

The women turn their attention to Ellen.

                    ELLEN ARMSTRONG (cont'd)
          Fifteen years ago a young woman sat
          and listened for hours at my mother
          Lucy's feet. She heard stories of
          the Wayandot's travels, the
          suffering and the wonderful joys
          they experienced. She was read
          letters from Susan B Anthony about
          the cause so dear to our hearts. I
          remember my mother encouraging this
          young woman to risk the untraveled
          path, choose law and help those
          that need a sharp and willing mind.

Ellen stands and places her hand on Lyda's shoulder.

                    ELLEN ARMSTRONG (cont'd)
          We the Wayandots are a matriarchal
          society... we tolerate proud,
          disobedient and ill-tempered woman.
          And so without another moment
          wasted listening to this ill-
          tempered woman I give you Lyda
          Burton Conley.

There is laughter and a warm welcome for Lyda.

                    LYDA
          As you are some of the most read
          woman in the State of Kansas I know
          you are keenly aware of our current
          battle with the government over the
          Huron Cemetery. What you may not
          know is that this is not the first,
          nor do I suspect the last.
                         (MORE)

                    LYDA (cont'd)
          Knowing I would be with you today I
          wanted to read something I cut out
          of the Wayandotte Gazette in May
          1890. It was a letter written to
          the newspaper by Ellen's mother,
          Lucy B. Armstrong and it was
          written in response to an effort by
          then senator Preston B. Plumb who
          claimed the cemetery was "a
          nuisance and that the Wayandots
          wished to have their ancestors
          moved to a more secluded location".
          Mrs. Armstrong wrote...

Lyda removes an old newspaper clipping and reads.

                    LYDA (cont'd)
          "To remove the burying-ground now
          would be to scatter the dust of the
          dead to the winds. What a
          sacrilege! I remember with
          reverence many of the good
          Wayandots buried there, and my
          heart protests against such
          desecration of that sacred ground.

Lyda places the article on the table, sips at her water and returns her attention to the women.

                    LYDA (cont'd)
          Yes my Mother and Father are buried
          there... and my grandparents as
          well, but this is not only the
          story of our ancestors... as I see
          woman here I do not know or have
          ever seen before. Where is your
          great grandmother buried? Perhaps
          not even in the United States. And
          what would you do if you were told
          men were at this moment taking
          picks and shovels to their resting
          place. Would you fight those that
          dare strike at your very soul. You
          are all here to seek a voice in
          your government... for the right to
          vote and hold office. My ancestors
          have no voice... they are helpless
          in their peace and so I, my sisters
          and those that support us must cry
          out. And I am taking that fight to
          the Supreme Court of The United
          States. And you should also know
          that I will be the first Native
          American Woman to do so.

The women stand and begin clapping and the applause continues as Lyda sits and begins to gather her things.

EXT. FORT CONLEY - AFTERNOON

Lena is picking up small sticks around the fort when Lyda calls out to her.

				LYDA
		We file tomorrow!

Lena smiles and continues picking up the small sticks. Lyda walks up to her.

				LYDA (cont'd)
		Did you hear what I said? I have
		the money to file. What is wrong
		with you?

				LENA
		More papers... We are blood, but we
		have a different view of this
		world. To me this is just more
		games that will be played. But
		played by smarter men than those
		here in Kansas. I think that today
		I realized something that I never
		saw before.

				LYDA
		Go on...

				LENA
		I realized that this will never
		end. We will spend the rest of our
		lives fighting this fight.

				LYDA
		Not if we win in the Supreme Court.

				LENA
		Yes, even then. How many treaties,
		contracts, promises must be broken
		to prove this to you. But I love
		you more than life and I will stand
		beside you in Washington. I just
		see so much more heartache ahead
		for us and it makes me sad.

Lyda puts her arm around Lena and kisses her cheek.

                    LYDA
          Let's go find Ida and give her the
          good news.

                    LENA
               (smiling)
          You are as crazy as they say I am.

                                        FADE OUT.

EXT. 1910 WASHINGTON, DC STREET DAY

Off the U.S. Capital building. Lyda looks over a list of
attorneys. She starts walking against the winter wind.

                    FLOATING VOICE   (V.O.)
          With the filing of Lyda's papers
          they were released from the day to
          day terror of the businessman that
          were seeking the land. But as Lena
          suspected the process was delayed
          for two years, hoping for sure that
          they would walk from the fight. In
          December nineteen hundred and nine
          Lyda received word that she was on
          the docket for January nineteen
          hundred and ten.

Lyda stops, checks her list and proceeds to a doorway. Her
knocks receive no response. A moment later she's inspired by
a sign directing her to enter.

INT. NORMAN BIGELOW'S OFFICE - CONTINUOUS

Lyda opens the door and enters a reception area. NORMAN
BIGELOW'S SECRETARY, at least seventy years old looks up.

                    NORMAN BIGELOW'S SECRETARY
          Can I help you, Miss?

                    LYDA
          I have interest in arguing before
          the Supreme Court. I'm in need of
          someone to vouch for my character.

                    NORMAN BIGELOW'S SECRETARY
          I've been Mr. Bigelow's secretary
          for fifty-one years and I don't
          know you, so I would imagine he
          doesn't either. If you would like
          to hire Mister Bigelow, that might
          be the wisest.

LYDA
I am a lawyer and a member of the
Kansas Bar.

NORMAN BIGELOW'S SECRETARY
Kansas? That's right, it's a state
now.

LYDA
Is it possible to speak with Mr.
Bigelow?

NORMAN BIGELOW (O.S.)
This way, young lady.

Lyda turns to see NORMAN BIGELOW, a man in his eighties, wheelchair-bound, roll himself out of the doorway. Lyda enters and sits. Norman wheels himself to her side, forgoing the formality of his desk.

NORMAN BIGELOW (cont'd)
She's a little protective of her
boss. The fact that we've been
married for fifty years just adds
to her tenacity. I'm Norman
Bigelow.

Lyda extends her hand.

LYDA
Lyda Conley. I need your help.

NORMAN BIGELOW
Conley v. Ballinger. Secretary of
the Interior, not bad.

LYDA
I'd sue God Almighty himself if I
thought it would help.

NORMAN BIGELOW
Something tells me you would. I no
longer get the court schedule,
however I've heard a spattering of
talk. Suing God Almighty might be
easier.

LYDA
I've been told that before.

NORMAN BIGELOW
You know I can't vouch for you, so
how else can I be of help.

                    LYDA
          There are over a hundred lawyers
          practicing before the court. I've
          met with over thirty-five and not
          one will help me.

                    NORMAN BIGELOW
          And you will meet the same fate
          with the remaining sixty-five. It's
          not your character they won't vouch
          for, it's your femininity... As a
          man with two daughters it shames me
          to say so.

                    LYDA
          Is it solely the fact that I am a
          woman?

                    NORMAN BIGELOW
          There are other factors. I'm
          certain your Indian heritage is the
          death blow to your efforts.

                    LYDA
          And what am I to do?

                    NORMAN BIGELOW
          What you've known since your first
          day in law class. You will argue
          pro se. As a citizen, not a lawyer.
          And the mere fact that you are
          before the Court vouches for your
          character. You are a citizen of the
          United States.

                    LYDA
          Thank you, Mr. Bigelow.

Lyda gets up and walks out of Norman's office.

INT. 1910 SUPREME COURT BUILDING - DAY

A black robe rests on an oak hanger as a hand reaches in and picks a small white speck from the shoulder.

INT. HOTEL ROOM - SAME

A female hand reaches up and takes a dress from a hanger.

INT. SUPREME COURT BUILDING - SAME

Papers are gathered from a desk and placed under another robed arm.

INT. HOTEL ROOM - SAME

Lyda reaches for a her papers resting on a table. She stops as she notices her hand shaking. She stands for a moment and watches the trembling, then closing her eyes, slips her other hand over the one that is shaking bringing it to her stomach, she doubles over.

INT. SUPREME COURT BUILDING - SAME

A single Justice looks out a large window into the sunlight beyond. A second Justice places an arm on his shoulder and they both turn, their stern faces drifting into shadow.

INT. HOTEL ROOM - SAME

Lyda is still bent over in front of her hotel window. Lena places her hand on Lyda's shoulder. Lyda turns and Lena hands her the court papers.

INT. SUPREME COURTROOM - DAY

The courtroom is packed with onlookers, lawyers, and the press. A murmur begins in the courtroom as Lena and Lyda step out from the covered doorway.

The two sisters step forward and an audible gasp escapes in the room, followed by whispers and a few stifled laughs. They continue walking, their heads held high and take their seats at a long wooden table in front of the courtroom. The BAILIFF steps forward.

                    BAILIFF
     All rise. The Supreme Court of the
     United States is now in session.
     Their Honorable Justices presiding.

The Justices enter the courtroom and as they sit, the courtroom follows. Lena pulls on Lyda's arm.

                    LYDA
     Yes?

                    LENA
          It's says there that he is the
          Chief. I'm not impressed if he's
          the Chief.

Everyone looks up at JUSTICE OLIVER WENDELL HOLMES. As the
Justice speaks and calls the names of the parties involved.

                    JUSTICE OLIVER WENDELL HOLMES
          The matter before the court today,
          January 14, 1910, is that of Conley
          v. Ballinger. Miss Lyda Burton
          Conley appears for the appellant.
          Solicitor General Bowers and Mr.
          Barton Corneau for appellees. In
          addition to the Secretary of the
          Interior Ballinger, Mr. Horace B.
          Durant, Mr. Thomas B. Walker and
          Mr. William A. Simpson,
          Commissioners are also named. Are
          the parties ready to proceed?

Lyda stands and quickly scoops up a handful of papers.

                    LYDA
          Yes, Your Honor.

                    JUSTICE OLIVER WENDELL HOLMES
          Then please begin.

                    LYDA
          I always...

Lyda nervously clears her throat.

                    LYDA (cont'd)
          I always knew I would be the one to
          tell this story. A story that
          begins with the first of the
          peaceful warriors, my grandmother,
          Little Bird Zane. Who with her
          people were forced to sell their
          birthright in the east and taken by
          the government to the promised land
          of Kansas. And so, at the age of
          sixteen, she discovered the
          sweetness of love and the bitter
          taste of life lost, all in the year
          eighteen-forty-three. There would
          be many buried at Wyandot Cemetery,
          some nine hundred others, known and
          unknown. The story of Little Bird
          is but one.
                         (MORE)

                    LYDA (cont'd)
          On the last day of her life, they
          found her at dawn, kneeling by the
          river, saying a final goodbye to
          her memories. Weak and dying, she
          climbed the hillside one last time
          to lie beside her love, LaSalle.
          The elders followed, and sitting a
          few feet away, heard her speak
          words never recorded on paper or
          spoken beyond our tribe until
          today. "I have come to be with you
          forever, and from this sacred
          ground we will not be moved." Were
          they the simple words of an Indian
          woman or the battle cry of a
          nation? I too desire that they bury
          me with my ancestors. To us, this
          is the most hallowed ground on
          earth. I cannot believe that the
          final resting place of my people is
          any less important than that of
          those buried here in our nations
          capital, who rest peacefully at
          Arlington National Cemetery.

Lyda places the final piece of paper down on the desk and
then is silent for a moment. Slowly, she raises her eyes to
meet those of the Justices.

                    LYDA (cont'd)
          I wonder how I will ever find rest
          if now I cannot find the words. A
          thought, something to put an end to
          this madness.

Lyda stops and closes her eyes. After a moment, she opens her
eyes and looks back at Lena. Then she turns again to the
Justices.

                    LYDA (cont'd)
          I rest my case beside the spirit of
          my ancestors. It is now up to you
          to form such a word or a thought in
          your decision. I leave you only
          with this. Who will watch over you
          when you have joined your
          ancestors?

INT. RANDOLPH JOHNSON'S OFFICE - DAY

Johnson throws his arm across his desk sending papers, pens
and a porcelain statue that breaks into pieces.

> RANDOLPH JOHNSON
> Supreme Court Decision!

Federal Marshal #3 bends to pick up the statue.

> RANDOLPH JOHNSON (cont'd)
> Leave it! Now listen to me and you are to do what I tell you or I swear you'll be serving chow to inmates at Leavenworth the rest of your life!

Randolph is flushed with rage.

> RANDOLPH JOHNSON (cont'd)
> You are going to meet a hundred soldiers at dawn tomorrow. They will be waiting by the library.

> FEDERAL MARSHAL#3
> I have plenty of men.

> RANDOLPH JOHNSON
> Shut your mouth! That god forsaken shack is built again. They're not women... they're carpenters from hell! I don't care how you do it, but I want it torn down again and guards posted so it won't get built, again.

> FEDERAL MARSHAL#3
> Okay.

> RANDOLPH JOHNSON
> You're Damn right Okay! I am suppose to buy that land in two weeks and get my foundations in before the ground freezes. Now get the hell out of here and you better take care of this issue tomorrow.

The Federal Marshal leaves the office.

> RANDOLPH JOHNSON (cont'd)
> Margaret!

Randolph's secretary enters the room and looks at the mess.

                    RANDOLPH JOHNSON (cont'd)
          Get someone to clean this up. Then
          call the editor over at the Kansan
          and get me a reporter over to that
          Indian shack at dawn. I want the
          world to know this is over!

EXT. FORT CONLEY - DAWN

A mist floats just above the grass and as the faint light of
day makes its way across the cemetary a lone figure walks
slowly toward Fort Conley.

The fence has been rebuilt and the fort stands erect. Federal
Marshal #3 stops fifty feet from the shack.

                    FEDERAL MARSHAL#3
          Attention in there! You have five
          minutes to vacate that shack or you
          will be forcibly removed!

He waits and there seems to be no movement.

                    FEDERAL MARSHAL#3 (CONT'D) (cont'd)
          I know you can hear me. I said you
          have four minutes to vacate that
          shack or you will be forcibly
          removed!

He waits again and there is no movement from Fort Conley.

                    FEDERAL MARSHAL#3 (cont'd)
          This is your final warning! You
          must leave now.

The door to the fort opens and Lena and Lyda step outside,
the shotgun in Lena's hand. Lena raises the shotgun toward
the Marshal.

The Federal Marshal just raises his hand as he walks toward
them. Over the hill behind him a sea of blue soldiers walks
in a line that spreads across the cemetary from end to end.
In unison they walk toward the Marshal.

They are three deep across the cemetary when they stop just a
few feet behind him and twenty feet from the fence. The
soldiers raise their rifles.

Lena and Lyda stand their ground.

Ida steps out of the doorway. She has draped a large American
Flag around her body so that she is engulfed in it. The
Soldiers eyes widen.

Ida walks forward, reaches out and placing her hand on the tip of the shotgun so that Lena will lower it. The shotgun now rests at Lena's side and Ida steps in front of her sisters protecting them with her flag draped body.

> IDA
> You boys in Blue might as well pull the trigger and fill this American Flag with bullet holes... kill me this very moment as that is the only way you'll touch a single blade of grass in this hallowed place.

The stand off continues as the soldiers rifles remain poised on the sisters.

> PHOTOGRAPHER (O.C.)
> Don't move!

Everyone turns toward the voice. He takes the photo.

> KANSAN REPORTER
> You got it?

> PHOTOGRAPHER
> Sure did.

The KANSAN REPORTER, notebook in hand stands ready to write.

> KANSAN REPORTER
> Okay... we're good.

The Photographer runs off.

Federal Marshall #3 turns to the soldiers.

> FEDERAL MARSHAL#3
> That's it. We're done here.

He walks through the soldiers who part so he can get by. They begin to follow him. Ida wraps her flag around Lyda and Lena and they all walk back into Fort Conley.

EXT. 1843 WYANDOT KANSAS VILLAGE - DAY

Word has spread that Little Bird is returning from the woods and the entire village has assembled to greet her.

> LITTLE BIRD
> Haywannen hatentaron onnionkaraye. Ethentronkwi eyontahkwi, ywatistakwandi.
> (MORE)

                    LITTLE BIRD (cont'd)
          Onhwa ekh'onyiondaon. Tsaten
          teweonyiondechrawache.
          Tetsionywaraskawache. Ndio
          haywannen hiehierandi.
          **(Your chief is lying on the high
          ridge where he will remain for all
          eternity. This I promise you. This
          is now our home and no one will
          ever move us from this land. We
          move no more! Come, your chief
          awaits his tribe.)**

INT. RANDOLPH JOHNSON'S HOME - MORNING

Johnson opens the papers to see Ida on the cover in all her American Flag glory and Lyda and Lena standing behind her. Randolph reads a few lines and then throws the papers across the kitchen of his home.

INT. RANDOLPH JOHNSON'S OFFICE - NIGHT

Johnson sits behind his desk as a group of ten thugs sit and lean around the office.

                    RANDOLPH JOHNSON
          I'm done playing by the rules. Are
          you clear about the result I want.

                    THUG #1
          Ah ugh.

                    RANDOLPH JOHNSON
          Here.

Randolph hands the Thug a handful of dollars. The other half you can pick up tomorrow.

Lighting strikes and thunder rolls in the distance.

EXT. HURON CEMETARY - NIGHT

Darkness prevails as wind driven rain pelts a small wooden shack. Dark figures begin to appear and surround the small structure. In one movement they pounce and with metal hand tools catching the faint light attack the structure. Boards are ripped out and thrown aside.

The door to the shack bursts open and two figures, their long hair and dresses mixing together as they tackle the bodies in front of them.

Rain, mud, cursing and bodies mix in a hysterical dance around the shack.

DARK FIGURE #1
What the hell was that!

DARK FIGURE #2
Over there...look out.

A board slaps the water as DF #1 rolls out of the way.

A woman's hair is pulled and she falls forward into the mud. From the blacked face white teeth glow as they find their mark in DF # 3 arm.

DARK FIGURE #3
They're eating me!

The Dark Figures wrestle the women to their feet and as the women kick and claw the men hold them tight as other men continue the devastation on the shack.

The red and white flash of a shotgun is followed a split second later by the thunderous clap as it rips in front of the bodies.

Everyone freezes as the men release the women and run off. The rain begins to wash away the mud from the womens' faces to reveal Lyda and Lena. Standing to the side, shotgun still at the ready is a smiling Ida.

FLOATING VOICE (V.O.)
That was the last the Sisters heard of Randolph Johnson or anyone else for a while. Their reputation kept buyers away even if the Supreme Court would not. Senator Curtis kept his word to join the fight and on February 13, 1913 Congress approved legislation that both repealed the part of the Indian Appropriation Act of 1906 authorizing the sale of the Huron Cemetery, but recommended that the cemetery become a national monument. Years would pass with only mild skirmishes but they were always on guard.

EXT. 1843 WYANDOT CEMETARY - LATER

Little Bird holds Eliza and watches families bring the bodies of their loved ones across the river by the hill;

the Missouri River. They climb up the hill to the ridge where LaSalle died overlooking Kansas and Missouri Rivers. They start to dig graves to bury them. Huron Cemetery is established.

EXT. 1930 HURON CEMETARY

Lena, now 66, is picking up tree branches that have fallen around the cemetary. A survey team of three men with their equipment stand off to the side.

SURVEYOR #1
You go.

SURVEYOR #2
We picked straws... you lost.

SURVEYOR #3
What is wrong with you two...

Surveyor #3 lets his equipment fall to the ground and walks toward Lena. As he gets ten feet away Lena turns and holds a large stick as a weapon.

SURVEYOR #3 (cont'd)
Take it easy.

LENA
Now why would I do that?

SURVEYOR #3
We're not bothering anybody.

LENA
Yes you are.

SURVEYOR #3
We'll be done in a few hours.

LENA
With what? Setting the stage to carve a few more feet away from our land. I know what you do.

SURVEYOR #3
We work for the city. We're just doing our job.

LENA
You do the devils work.

Surveyor #3 walks off to join his coworkers.

                    SURVEYOR #1
               Here comes the Mayor.

The MAYOR of Kansas City dressed in a suit and tie walks past
the Surveyors and nods,

                    MAYOR
               Lena... You need to let these men
               do their work.

                    LENA
               Miss Conley!

                    MAYOR
               You can't keep doing this... Miss
               Conley. There is progress in the
               world and we need to fix these
               sidewalks.

                    LENA
               Progress... Yes progressively
               taking this land. I am giving you a
               chance to save your soul by leaving
               us alone. If you stay I will be
               forced to curse you to live a life
               of misery.

The Mayor opens his mouth to speak and then just turns and
walks away motioning for the surveyors to follow him.

INT. 1930 VICE PRESIDENTS OFFICE - TWENTY YEARS LATER

Vice President Charles Curtis sits behind his desk reading a
memo when his secretary knocks softly and enters.

                    CHARLES CURTIS V.P. SECRETARY
               Mister Vice President.

                    CHARLES CURTIS
               Yes.

                    CHARLES CURTIS V.P. SECRETARY
               You have an unscheduled visitor.

                    CHARLES CURTIS
               Then schedule them.

                    CHARLES CURTIS V.P. SECRETARY
               She says that she has come to say
               thank you for something you did for
               her family years ago. I have to say
               I don't think she is leaving
               without seeing you.

CHARLES CURTIS
Intense eyes and well spoken?

CHARLES CURTIS V.P. SECRETARY
That would be her.

Charles Curtis nods and his secretary exits. Lyda, 56 enters the office. Everything they experienced is relived in a moment. Charles stands and makes his way around the desk. Lyda extends her hand and Charles takes it.

LYDA
I have followed your political rise and was never surprised by your success.

CHARLES CURTIS
Nor I yours.

Charles motions for Lyda to sit but she remains standing.

CHARLES CURTIS (cont'd)
How are your sisters?

LYDA
They like all of us are getting older, but in their eyes I still see the spirit that stood against the greatest odds.

CHARLES CURTIS
You were their rock.

LYDA
No. It was the ones that you never saw. The children helping their parents drag lumber and tools. The mothers that brought us food, the husbands that built the fence... twenty times. They were the rock for us all. And you... is your family well?

CHARLES CURTIS
My children are well, scattered across the states, but my wife Annie died five years ago.

An emotion passes between them and is gone.

CHARLES CURTIS (cont'd)
So... Do you have official business in Washington?

                    LYDA
          No... I came to see you. There have
          been few men in my life whose words
          meant more to me than yours. I knew
          from the moment we met that you
          were special, and during that most
          difficult time you never spoke a
          word you did not honor. I did not
          want this lifetime to pass without
          you knowing that you, as much as
          anyone saved our Huron Cemetery.

                    CHARLES CURTIS
          I...

Lyda raises her hand to silence Charles who can only smile at
her spirit.

                    LYDA
          You must hear this... You were
          called like the great warriors
          before you to help us. You heard
          the call and that is what I knew
          when we met. As much as I wanted it
          you had not been sent to join me in
          romance, but to join me in the
          fight. You will forever be the man
          in my life and for that I was truly
          blessed.

Lyda rises. Charles, looks as Lyda walks to the door. She
turns.

                    LYDA (cont'd)
              (smiling)
          Oh and one more thing... You're one
          of the few men that has ever seen
          me naked and I'm just pleased that
          it was then and not now.

Lyda walks out.

EXT. 1933 HURON CEMETARY - DAY

A work crew with pick axes and shovels stand idle looking
into a trench near the cemetery.

                    WORK CREW MEMBER #1
          Please get out of there.

He leans in and extends his hand. Lyda, crosses her arms over
her chest.

                    WORK CREW MEMBER #1 (CONT'D) (cont'd)
          They sent for the police.

                    LYDA
          Young man I've stared down a
          hundred U.S. Soldiers, stood toe to
          toe with Federal Marshals do you
          really believe I'm fearful of the
          Kansas City police?

The Crew Member steps away and is replaced by a Police
Captain.

                    POLICE CAPTAIN #2
          Aren't you a little old to be
          causing trouble?

                    LYDA
          I certainly hope not.

                    POLICE CAPTAIN #2
          Miss Conley if you don't come up
          from there and let these men finish
          their job. I am personally going to
          come down and get you. Then I'm
          going to take you to jail.

Lyda looks right into the Captains eyes.

                    POLICE CAPTAIN #2 (cont'd)
          How did she get in there.

                    WORK CREW MEMBER #1
          She jumped.

The Police Captain looks for a way down.

                    POLICE CAPTAIN
          Give me a ladder.

The workman scramble. He makes his way down the ladder and
into the trench. His feet land and Lyda is gone. He looks up
to see Lyda running away down the trench.

HOLD ON LYDA RUNNING.

1936 VICE PRESIDENT CHARLES CURTIS DIED AFTER A FAILED RUN
FOR PRESIDENT.

1946 LYDA CONLEY DIED AT THE AGE OF 72. SHE WAS ROBBED WHILE
RETURNING HOME FROM THE CEMETARY. THE THIEF GOT AWAY WITH
THIRTY CENTS.

1948 IDA CONLEY DIED TWO YEARS AFTER HER SISTER LYDA.

LENA KEPT HER DAILY VIGIL WALKING EACH DAY TO HURON CEMETERY PROTECTING THE SISTERS SHE LOVED SO MUCH.

1958 LENA DIED AT THE AGE OF 94.

FADE TO BLACK.

> FLOATING VOICE (V.O.)
> It would be many years after Lena took her last breath in nineteen fifty eight that the fight for Huron Cemetery would finally end.

EXT. HURON CEMETARY CURRENT TIME - DAY

Slowly coming into focus as the words are spoken is the National Historic Site marker.

> FLOATING VOICE (V.O.)
> The government that had tried in vain to take this sacred ground had in the end protected it from itself and others by declaring the cemetery a National Historic Site. The Conley sisters had won and finally rest in peace.

Words appear on screen.

ONHWA SKEWENDA, EHTE. - Floating Voice.

(YOU ARE NOW THE BEARER OF MY WORDS.)

CREDITS ROLL OVER REAL HISTORICAL PHOTOS OF:

FORT CONLEY

IDA CONLEY

LENA CONLEY

LYDA CONLEY

CHARLES CURTIS

CURRENT DAY HURON CEMETARY.

"YOU TRESPASS AT YOUR OWN PERIL."

You Trespass at Your Own Peril!

THE STORY OF THE THREE CONLEY SISTERS, WHO FOUGHT WITH SHOTGUNS, AXES AND THE LAW TO SAVE THEIR ANCESTORS INDIAN BURIAL GRAVES.

"My father's spirit came to me in a dream and was unhappy and I knew what that meant," Helena said. "The dead want this holy place defended and it will be."

"As soon as the Conley sisters realized that the sale was pending they announced that they would protect the graves of their ancestors, if necessary, with shotguns. Forthwith, they marched to the cemetery and threw up a 6 by 8 one room frame shack hard by the ancestral resting place and moved in."

"…while Lyda fought her battle in the courts, her sister Helena, who prefers the name Helene, guarded the fort, keeping things trim in the burial ground, felling dead trees with an ax while awed bystanders admired the play of her muscles, resenting intrusion by roaming holiday makers. Because of the intrusions, the sisters finally wired the cemetery gates together and put up a sign: "You Trespass at Your Own Peril."

Whispers Like Thunder, the movie   Contact: LuisMoroProductions.com 310.728.0851

Three Sisters Defense of Cemetery

Lasts Nearly Forty Years

"I will go to Washington and personally defend it... If I do not then there is no cemetery in this land safe from sale, at the will of the government."[1] Lyda Burton Conley

Friday June 7, 1946

Kansas City Times By Henry Van Brunt

Recent Death of Miss Lyda Conley Recalls Long Series of Outbreaks and Defiance of Law by Women Who Built Shack on Indian Burial Ground in Heart of Kansas City, Kansas and Lived beside Graves of Ancestors.

The death on May 28 of the most aggressive of the three Huron park Conley sisters--Lyda Burton Conley--at the age of 72 sent the writer on an adventurous trek through the files of the Star, picking up the back trail of what you might call the one woman Indian mutiny of Kansas City, Kansas.

The file of clippings arranged chronologically, measures more than half an inch in thickness and covering a period of forty years, come October, represents the reportorial activity of perhaps scores of reporters, many of whom, obviously had no realization of the venerable tenure of the subject they were handling. For instance, it was hardly fair to refer to Miss Conley
in 1928 as having "recently cause trouble in Huron cemetery" when that stubborn champion of Indian burial rights had then been at it formerly a score of years. Trouble was her prerogative; she thrived on trouble...And, as far as the writer is concerned, they can take all the clippings and file them in the Zane family lot as an enduring monument to pertinacity and publicity.

As background for the Conley epic, it is necessary to bring up the Wyandot migration and the big rain of 1844. The Wyandotte's came to the confluence of the Missouri and Kaw rivers (July 28 and 31 in 1843).and settled in the Westport area until the Delaware sold them thirty six sections and gave them three sections in memory of friendship what is now Wyandotte County. Records are lacking, but it is reliably reported to have rained forty days and forty nights in 1844. Floods filled the whole area of what is now the Central Industrial district, an epidemic of small pox followed and between 200 and 300 (according to the Star account) Indians died. They were buried in the Huron Park also known as Wyandot National Cemetery.

That is the basis for the Conley sisters; defense of the Indian burial ground. Their mother was buried there (their sister Sarah) and, these, ancestors further back (actually many cousins, Uncles, and Aunts; and their Grandmother, Hannah Zane.

The revolt of the three sisters, started in the summer of 1907 as a result of plans broached the previous year for purchase by the city of the Huron cemetery, Congress, having authorized its sale by the secretary of the Interior in 1905 (1906) .

As soon as the Conley sisters realized that the sale was pending they announced that they would protect the graves of their ancestors, if necessary, with shotguns. Forthwith, they marched to the cemetery and threw up a 6 by 8 one room frame shack hard by the ancestral resting place and moved in. H.B. Durante, Indian commissioner commented that it was a unique situation and washed his hands of it, suggesting that it was up to the Department of Justice and Federal troops.

Troops never were called to eject the sisters, who defended their cemetery fort through 1907, 1908, 1909, and through the summer of 1910. Throughout this period, Lyda prepared herself for legal action by an assiduous study of law books, the better to contest the government order. When the battle began the new Carnegie library stood in the center of the square, the new Brund hotel stood at one corner, and on another preparations were being made for the reconstruction of the Masonic Temple, destroyed by fire.

It was William Rodekepf, paving contractor, who won the distinction of the first actual encounter with the sisters by tearing down a fence which the Conleys with help from their tribal brothers and sisters erected between the cemetery and the temple site.

The sisters rebuilt the fence, and the contractor's men tore it down again. Again Lyda rebuilt it in defiance of an injunction obtained by the Masonic bodies, and it was again laid low. The writer took a pencil and tried to figure the number of times the fence was destroyed and rebuilt during a fort night in the winter of 1907, but gave it up. On one occasion the sisters defended their fence with sticks and stones

Through this early period, the rightful ownership of the cemetery remained in doubt-- unless it could be said that the Conleys owned it by right of possession. There was a federal order to remove the bodies to Quindaro cemetery, but it was qualified in such a way as to leave grounds for suits in the federal courts, and Lyda Conley took full advantage of this opportunity, supported by women's clubs and others with whom sentiment outweighed commercialism and twentieth century progress.

And while Lyda fought her battle in the courts, her sister Helena, who prefers the name Helene, guarded the fort, keeping things trim in the burial ground, felling dead trees with an ax while awed bystanders admired the play of her muscles, resenting intrusion by roaming holiday makers. Because of the intrusions, the sisters finally wired the cemetery gates together and put up a sign: **"You Trespass at Your Own Peril."** None disregarded it.

Lyda Conley was admitted to the Kansas bar in 1910 and in the course of her fight against removal of the Indian graves, made several trips to Washington. She is said to have been the first woman lawyer (actually Indian Woman Lawyer) to plead before the United States Supreme Court.

On July 29, while Lyda and her sisters were in Wyandotte County District Court hearing arguments in the last legal step they took to hold the cemetery, the United States marshal and his deputies entered the cemetery and destroyed the "fort" and an injunction was issued forbidding the sisters to rebuild it.

Finally, in August, 1912, the House Indian Affairs Committee in Washington favorably reported a bill prohibiting the removal of the cemetery--the first ray of hope the sisters had in their fight. However, they did not definitely settle the affair, and the sisters still held their ground among the graves.

There is a little item in May of 1918 recording the fact that Lyda pulled up some stakes driven near the cemetery by city surveyors, bruised and scratched three detectives (!!??) who dragged her to police headquarters. She was fined $100 for destroying city property.

In the intervening years, Lyda--her case won insofar as sale of the property was concerned--the government having agreed to keep the cemetery "improved" (by entering into a 1918 contract with the City of KCK to FOREVER maintain, protect and provide lighting and police protection to the cemetery) confined her activities to a watchful guardianship, which included care of the birds
and squirrels in the cemetery. On the coldest winter days she would leave her home at 1816 North Third street and carry water and nuts to the squirrels.

Then in June, 1937, wielding a broomstick, she chased some people from the cemetery. A young judge, perhaps not cognizant of the fact that Lyda had never been in jail in all the twenty-six years of her defiance of the authorities, gave her choice of a $10 fine for disturbing the peace or a 10
day jail sentence.

Proudly she served the sentence. The item of June 16, 1937 headed "Miss Lyda Conley Leaves Jail, (KC Star?) was the last printed appearance of Lyda until the notice of her death and of her burial on May 31.

Whispers Like Thunder, the movie   Contact: LuisMoroProductions.com 310.728.0851

Huron Cemetery
Curse May Play Role In Cemetery Combat
Sunday May 17, 1959   Kansas City Times   by Jay Lastelic

The Wyandot Indian curse, reputed never to have failed will be tested again tomorrow morning before a congressional committee.

No mention of the curse will be made by a delegation going to Washington in an attempt to save the historic Huron Indian Cemetery in Kansas City, Kansas, but the threat remains.

In the 116 year old burying ground of the Wyandot lies Miss Helena Conley, self-styled sorceress of the tribe. While she lived, two presidents, members of Congress, mayors, professional persons, policemen and others had the curse placed upon them. Now her tombstone proclaims to all:

"CURSED BE THE VILLAIN THAT MOLEST THEIR GRAVES"

Since 1890 there have been periodic battles in Congress and in the courts including the U.S. Supreme Court for preservation of the 2-acre tract in downtown Kansas City, Kansas. But the odds were never greater against those who today would save the site from commercialization.

Led by Mayor Paul F. Mitchum and George Zane, Chief of the Wyandots in this area the protesters are fighting the sale by the Oklahoma Wyandots who pushed a bill through Congress and gained possession of the land. Armed with letters, telegrams and petitions with more than 5,000 signatures, the delegation will present legal and historical data to the House committee on
interior and insular affairs in a hearing tomorrow morning. Was even Newell A. George sponsor of bills that would prevent the sale and make the area a national historic shrine victim of the curse?

Before going to Washington he made a speech in which he suggested removal of the cemetery to another spot as a possible solution to the periodic legal battle. Within the month George was in a motor car accident and as he lay critically injured in an emergency his surgeon scolded: "I told you to leave that cemetery alone."

Errett P. Scrivner, George's predecessor in Congress from the Second Kansas district fought for the cemetery for years and knew all the legends about the curse. Was he a victim?

The sleeper bill for the sale of the cemetery passed in his last term. It provided a campaign issue. Scrivner was dubbed a "Rip Van Winkle Congressman, Sleepy in the Teepee". He lost the election.

Whispers Like Thunder, the movie   Contact: LuisMoroProductions.com 310.728.0851

The deaths and affliction of many prominent persons were attributed by Miss Conley to the effectiveness of the curse.

The Republican king maker, Sen. Preston B. Plumb, a founder of the city of Emporia, Kansas introduced a resolution in 1890 to sell the property. His death a year later was described as "untimely" and attributed to "overwork which brought on an attack of apoplexy."

George Schwabe, representative in Congress from Tulsa who always worked for the sale, collapsed and died while playing solitaire. Another Democratic congressman, Joseph Taggart, from Wyandotte County proposed the bill which passed in Senate in 1916, and was defeated in his third-term bid that year.

President Theodore Roosevelt, who signed the bill authorizing the sale, was the successful Republican candidate for President and was defeated as the Progressive party candidate.

These were the stories that Miss Conley related to those who visited her in her worn home at 1704 North Third St. in a Negro district of the city.

Miss Conley said the power of the curse was transmitted to her by a woman of the tribe, known as a witch who is buried in the cemetery. "She asked me," Miss Conley used to tell, "if I would rather have power or money. I said power."

She remembered that it was after the death of her mother and father, an Englishman of means, that she and her sisters, Ida and Lyda, took up their vigil over the graves after learning the land was about to be sold.

On July 25, 1907 they built a 6x8 foot frame structure and placed a fence of iron spikes around it. The three sisters stood armed with their father's musket (actually a double barreled shotgun). Promptly, it was named "Fort Conley."

"My father's spirit came to me in a dream and was unhappy and I knew what that meant," Helena said. "The dead want this holy place defended and it will be."

For almost five years the sisters kept their vigil, defying the United States Marshal, policemen or anyone who tried to interfere. Lyda, who became a lawyer, contended they were "beneficiary owners and users of an estate in the cemetery" made by the 1855 treaty that set the land aside for a burial ground.

Helena Conley was the last survivor of the family. She died September 15, 1958, at the age of 94. Often she wondered about her longevity.

"Our body has to return to mother earth and our spirit to God who made it," she said. "We don't know how we came here, nor why, nor where we go. I don't know why I'm left in this God-forsaken place. It's a cursed world – a separation from God."

Whispers Like Thunder, the movie   Contact: LuisMoroProductions.com 310.728.0851

A Defender of Huron Cemetery Dies at 72

(Transcriptions are presented without changes except to improve readability.)

Miss Lyda Burton Conley, who became locally famous as the protector of Huron cemetery, burial place of the Wyandot Indians, died at 6 o'clock this morning at the home, 1704 North Third, where she and her two sisters, Misses Ida and Helena Conley, have lived all their lives. She was 72 years old.

Miss Conley first caught the community's attention when in 1906 she instituted injunction proceedings against disposal of the cemetery, burial place of her mother's ancestors. The long struggle that she and her sisters maintained in defense of this famous landmark was the highlight of her picturesque career.

In the treaty of 1855 by which the Wyandots ceded their tribal lands back to the United States, to be subdivided and deeded to the members in severalty, it was the intent of the framers to preserve the historic old burial ground. The treaty contains such a proviso.

Sought Removal
In spite of that guarantee numerous attempts were made to sell the sacred plot and remove the bodies to Quindaro cemetery. In 1890 U.S. Sen. Preston B. Plumb introduced a resolution providing for sale of the cemetery. The act set out that the cemetery was a "nuisance" and that a majority of the then living Wyandots preferred that their ancestors be moved to a more secluded spot. The senator estimated the value of the cemetery at $100,000.

But local protest was so vociferous that the resolution failed of passage. Later the agitation was revived until congress finally enacted a bill to sell the cemetery and a commission was named to negotiate the deal. At this juncture Miss Conley started injunction proceedings and the sisters Conley erected their famous fort in the cemetery to fend off all invaders. The fort was a small frame building in which the conleys resided and maintained a day and night vigilance. They were armed, according to tradition.

Although the defense of the cemetery was carried to the highest court in the land, invariably all of the courts sustained congress in authorizing the secretary of the interior to make the sale, according to a local history book.

No Buyer Found
But until this day no buyer ever was found for the cemetery and it still is directed by the Bureau of Indian Affairs of the interior Department - and the Conley sisters. They have always contended that the original treaty guaranteed perpetual preservation of the cemetery, and that a subsequent federal order declared that it be held in trust for the Wyandots, with the city of Kansas City, Kansas as trustee.

Whispers Like Thunder, the movie   Contact: LuisMoroProductions.com 310.728.0851

Miss Conley again physically "held her ground" in June of 1929, when the city began excavation for a new retaining wall on the west side of Huron cemetery. Excavation for the new wall was completed except for a strip about 5 feet wide, 7 feet long and 20 feet deep, when she sat with her feet hanging over the ledge, defying workmen and city officials to continue digging.

She declared that the construction would invade five feet of sacred burial ground. "I'll fight this encroachment as long as I live," she was quoted as saying, "in my sentiments and feelings I am an Indian. When Miss Conley began tossing clods back in the trench she was forcibly removed from the ground and taken to jail where she stayed in preference to paying the $10 fine because she said she had done nothing wrong. Her appeal to Vice President Curtis was to no avail. Helena, better known as Lena, was also on the scene to reinforce her sister if necessary.

Built It Legally

Because the city was responsible for the maintenance of the park, the wall was legally built against the will of the Conley sisters.

The parents of the Conley sisters, Andrew S. Conley and Eliza Zane, are both buried in the Huron cemetery, where Miss Conley will be buried. Eliza Zane was part Indian, according to Miss Conley, and their father was a white man.

Since 1906, Lyda Conley had not ceased to patrol the cemetery. She could be seen each day en route to the cemetery, up Third Street to Everett, on Everett to Sixth to Minnesota to the cemetery. Her route seldom varied and she often took with her garden implements to aid her in cleaning the cemetery. She was a member of the Seventh Street Methodist church.

The body was taken to the Gibson funeral home where funeral arrangements are not complete.

Helena Conley, Lyda Conley, and cousin Nina Craig, ca. 1930.

Lyda Burton Conley at her 1902 graduation from the Kansas City College of Law.

HELENA CONLEY
FLOATING-VOICE
WYANDOTTE NATIONAL BURYING GROUND
"CURSED BE THE VILLIAN THAT
MOLEST THEIR GRAVES"

IDA CONLEY
DEPARTED THIS LIFE
OCT. 6, 1948

ELIZA BURTON CONLEY
DEPARTED THIS LIFE MAY 28, 1946
ATTORNEY AT LAW
ONLY WOMAN EVER ADMITTED TO
THE UNITED STATES SUPREME COURT

Whispers Like Thunder, the movie Contact: LuisMoroProductions.com 310.728.0851

Whispers Like Thunder, the movie   Contact: LuisMoroProductions.com 310.728.0851

Whispers Like Thunder, the movie   Contact: LuisMoroProductions.com 310.728.0851

Whispers Like Thunder, the movie   Contact: LuisMoroProductions.com 310.728.0851

Made in the USA
San Bernardino, CA
30 November 2017